Nicholas A. Roes, PhD

Solutions
for the "Treatment-Resistant"
Addicted Client
Therapeutic Techniques
for Engaging Challenging Clients

D0778349

*Pre-publication
REVIEWS,
COMMENTARIES,
EVALUATIONS . . .*

"**T**his book is a gem! Dr. Roes teaches the reader how to offer hope to the hopeless, and he is amazingly adept at reframing, normalizing, and clarifying goals. If a chemical dependency counselor could have only one addictions book on his or her shelf, this should be it."

Raymond Restaino, MS, CSW-R
*Clinical Program Manager,
Sullivan County Alcohol
and Drug Abuse Services,
Liberty, NY*

"**A**t a time when the field of addictions treatment is faced with helping clients with challenging problems, Nicholas Roes has given us an optimistic book of solutions. In an easy style that shines with respect and empathy for clients, Dr. Roes synthesizes an extensive array of techniques and presents them in a clear, practical, and lively manner through case examples and practice exercises. Treatment providers will love this book: beginning counselors for its clarity and applicability; seasoned counselors for its wisdom and challenges to the status quo; and supervisors for its power as a teaching tool. It should be utilized in any undergraduate or graduate school of counseling. The book is a gem that belongs in every clinician's treasury."

Vince Treanor, MSEd, CASAC
*Senior Trainer, Training Unit,
New York State Office of Alcoholism
and Substance Abuse Services,
Albany*

NOTES FOR PROFESSIONAL LIBRARIANS
AND LIBRARY USERS

This is an original book title published by The Haworth Press, Inc. Unless otherwise noted in specific chapters with attribution, materials in this book have not been previously published elsewhere in any format or language.

CONSERVATION AND PRESERVATION NOTES

All books published by The Haworth Press, Inc. and its imprints are printed on certified pH neutral, acid free book grade paper. This paper meets the minimum requirements of American National Standard for Information Sciences-Permanence of Paper for Printed Material, ANSI Z39.48-1984.

Solutions
for the "Treatment-Resistant"
Addicted Client
Therapeutic Techniques
for Engaging Challenging Clients

HAWORTH Addictions Treatment
F. Bruce Carruth, PhD
Senior Editor

Solutions
for the "Treatment-Resistant" Addicted Client
Therapeutic Techniques
for Engaging Challenging Clients

Nicholas A. Roes, PhD

Routledge
Taylor & Francis Group
www.routledgementalhealth.com

Transferred to digital printing 2010 by Routledge

Routledge
Taylor and Francis Group
270 Madison Avenue
New York, NY 10016

Routledge
Taylor and Francis Group
2 Park Square
Milton Park, Abingdon
Oxon OX14 4RN

© 2002 by Nicholas A. Roes. All rights reserved. No part of this work may be reproduced or utilized in any form or by any means, electronic or mechanical, including photocopying, microfilm, and recording, or by any information storage and retrieval system, without permission in writing from the publisher.

The Haworth Press, Inc., 10 Alice Street, Binghamton, NY 13904-1580

Cover design by Anastasia Litwak.

PUBLISHER'S NOTE
Names and identifying information and details presented in case studies have been changed to protect the clients' identities.

Library of Congress Cataloging-in-Publication Data

Roes, Nicholas A.
    Solutions for the "treatment-resistant" addicted client : therapeutic techniques for engaging challenging clients / Nicholas A. Roes.
        p. cm.
    Includes bibliographical references and index.
    ISBN 0-7890-1120-4 (alk. paper)—ISBN 0-7890-1121-2 (soft : alk. paper)
    1. Drug abuse—Treatment. 2. Alcoholism—Treatment. I. Title.

RC564 .R634 2001
616.86'0651—dc21

2001016625

To the women of New Hope Manor,
from whom I have learned all that I share in this book

ABOUT THE AUTHOR

Nick Roes, PhD, is currently Executive Director of a residential substance abuse treatment facility in upstate New York, where he has spent the last twelve years testing and refining the techniques in this book.

Dr. Roes has appeared on hundreds of radio and television talk shows (including *Donahue* and *Good Morning, America*). He has written six previous books and more than one thousand published articles on a wide range of topics.

Dr. Roes earned his PhD from Westbrook University in addictions treatment, and he is certified by New York State as a Certified Alcohol and Substance Abuse Counselor (CASAC). He is also a Registered Addiction Specialist (RAS) and Criminal Justice Counselor (CJC). He has been an adjunct instructor for Marist College and a guest lecturer at Rutgers University. He is also a faculty member of the New York State Office of Alcohol and Substance Abuse Services Bureau of Workforce Development Training Unit and is a frequent presenter of workshops to fellow professionals.

CONTENTS

Special thanks to my editor, Dr. Bruce Carruth,
and to Dr. G. Martin Woodard, for their careful review
of my manuscript and many helpful suggestions

Introduction

The intent of this text is to broaden the range of therapeutic techniques at the disposal of practicing counselors and students. A great body of research (Hubble, Duncan, and Miller, 1999) suggests that one of the most important factors contributing to the success of any technique is that both client and counselor have confidence that it will work. The more different techniques we are comfortable with, the more likely we will be able to match our techniques with techniques our clients accept with enthusiasm and self-confidence.

Although many of the therapeutic techniques are associated with a particular school or treatment model, most are easily adapted to your current model. My original intent was to offer these techniques objectively, outside the context of any specific treatment approach. But I realized (with help from my editor) that it was impossible to present my suggestions completely free of any philosophical bias. While I don't consider myself to be married to any particular school or model, there is a philosophy or set of assumptions behind my suggestions. It's only fair that these are shared with the reader up front.

The context in which all these suggestions are best used is one of love and respect for the client. Although this is an ironic statement to make in the introduction of a book on therapeutic techniques, I believe it's not so important *what* counselors do as *how* they do it. Whatever techniques they choose to use, the most successful therapists from any school are perceived by their clients as warm, trustworthy, nonjudgmental, and empathic (Miller, Hubble, and Duncan, 1997). So a genuine respect for the client and a willingness to learn from the client are behind my suggestions for the use of any therapeutic technique.

Any technique is used most respectfully when the client is not only included in the process but also recognized by the therapist as the driving force behind all successful treatment outcomes. The client's active participation in treatment is a confirming sign that your approach is respectful. A passive or resistant client may be a warning sign that you are not successfully communicating your love and respect. So without the client's fully informed consent, the use of some techniques, such as intimidating, conditioning, hypnotizing, or medicating clients to change, is not respectful.

There is always the danger of using even the best techniques disrespectfully. I believe we disrespect our clients when we manipulate them, disregard their feelings and ideas, or attach to all their behavior that motive that best suits our model of addiction. It is a sign of respect when we are willing to adjust our model to suit the human being we have engaged in treatment, and it is disrespectful to twist the human being we have engaged in treatment to fit our model.

Not long ago, a young woman came to our drug treatment facility who had lost her family, lost her job, had no place to live, and recently tried to kill herself by inhaling automobile exhaust. She had been refused admission by another program, where she was told she "wasn't ready" for treatment.

How much readier for help could a person be? What the staff of that treatment program probably meant was that *they* were not ready to deal with *her.* Their model of addiction excluded the possibility of hope for a woman who was not yet ready to see things the way the staff wanted her to. Challenging addicted clients are often shunned by mental health professionals who aren't quite sure how to reach them. In other cases, these clients are admitted to treatment, but the notion that they are beyond help becomes a self-fulfilling prophecy.

We all find some clients more pleasant to work with than others. But we sometimes forget that it's often the clients who are the most annoying, obnoxious, and hard to deal with who need our help the most. We don't want to be like the bankers who won't lend out money unless people can prove they really don't need it! We need to do better for those who need us the most.

The Myth of Treatment Readiness

One thing that stands in our way is the myth of "treatment readiness." It's not the client's job to be ready for our preferred type of counseling. It's our job, as counselors, to provide the type of counseling the client is ready for, or refer the client to someone else.

Fifty or so years ago, heart attack victims died more frequently than they do today. In fifty years, techniques and technology have developed that make survival much more likely. It would be silly to say that heart patients were less ready for treatment fifty years ago. As new techniques and technology become available, doctors are "readier" for their patients.

Part of the myth of treatment readiness is the idea that some clients are "resistant" to treatment. Consider the possibility that clients don't create resistance, but counselors do. Clients and counselors both have agendas. The counselor's may be abstinence, while the client's may be staying out of jail. We create resistance when we insist on our own agenda, rather than cooperating with the client.

Solutions for the "Treatment-Resistant" Addicted Client focuses on how we can be readier for our most challenging clients, and how we might avoid creating resistance. It offers field-tested therapeutic techniques that will help you deal with hopeless clients, those referred to as "in denial," and mandated clients.

Hopelessness is often confused with resistance. Section I focuses on therapeutic techniques that have proved to be especially helpful to hopeless, pessimistic, and passive clients. Section II covers techniques especially helpful in dealing with clients considered to be in denial. Section III deals with mandated clients.

It is assumed that these chapters will be read in order, as references are often made to previous pages. So, even though you may deal exclusively with mandated clients, for example, don't skip the chapters on meeting the challenge of hopeless clients, or dealing with clients seen as in denial. Many mandated clients are also hopeless, or considered to be in denial, and the techniques in Sections I and II are often helpful with those mandated to treatment. These first three sections include a hands-on feature that provides an opportunity for the reader to practice the techniques, with suggestions for possible responses at the end of each section.

Section IV includes suggestions for ways to give your therapeutic message greater impact and break out of unproductive patterns of relating to your clients. Unlike the techniques in the first three sections, Section IV includes techniques that are to be used sparingly. Overuse will dilute their effectiveness, and there is the possibility that they can backfire if not handled properly. For this reason, we suggest these be used only when other techniques have been tried and have failed.

The final section is presented in a question and answer format, and addresses practical application, theoretical framework, and ethical concerns.

Most case studies involve clients in residential treatment at New Hope Manor (an all-female, residential substance abuse treatment center), though a few have been contributed by colleagues from other modalities. Of course, identifying information and other details have been changed to protect the identity of the clients.

The emphasis throughout the text is on providing practical ideas that you can put to work within the context of your current treatment approach. Beyond the brief explanation of the context in which I use these techniques, this book does not seek to convert you to a new treatment philosophy, nor ask you to give up the tools that have been working for you. I offer additional tools to add to your repertoire—tools I hope will make a difference in dealing with your most challenging clients.

The opinions expressed in this book are mine, and are not to be construed as those of New Hope Manor, Inc., their board of directors, or staff.

SECTION I:
MEETING THE CHALLENGE
OF HOPELESS CLIENTS

"Hopeless" is certainly not a label we wish to hang on our clients. It is used here to distinguish one group of challenging clients from other challenging clients, with the idea of encouraging a more, rather than less, individualized treatment approach.

Some challenging clients have an unrealistic and unfounded optimism, sometimes called denial. They may feel, despite what many others are telling them, that they will be "okay." Hopeless clients are unrealistically pessimistic about their future. Despite what they may be told by supportive family members or therapists, they can see no way out of their current difficulties. While some challenging clients have unrealistically high self-esteem and self-confidence, clients without hope have an unrealistically low self-esteem and very little self-confidence.

While some challenging clients seem to take the view, "nothing is *my* fault," hopeless clients are more likely to think "*everything* is my fault." Hopeless clients often accept the blame for the behavior of adults who abused them when they were children, for the marital problems of their parents, or for the infidelity of their spouses.

Some challenging clients only seek treatment because of external pressure. They come to see us when treatment is the lesser of two evils offered by a court, their employers, or their families. Hopeless clients may seek treatment because they have internalized their problems. They

---

A Comparison of Two Challenging Client Types

Clients "in Denial"	"Hopeless" Clients
• Unrealistically optimistic	• Unrealistically pessimistic
• Unrealistically high self-esteem and self-confidence	• Unrealistically low self-esteem and self-confidence
• Feel "nothing is my fault"	• Feel "everything is my fault"
• Seek treatment due to external pressure	• Seek treatment after internalizing problems
• Don't believe they need treatment; don't really want to change	• Don't believe treatment can help; don't believe they can change

---

feel fundamentally flawed, damaged goods with problems that they can't separate from themselves, much less solve.

Some clients, often mandated to treatment, present a challenge because they are convinced they can handle their own lives without a counselor's interference. Many hopeless clients are convinced their problems are unsolvable—even with the help of a treatment professional. Finally, many challenging clients appear to be resistant because they don't really want to change in the ways others want them to change. Perhaps hopeless clients are viewed as resistant because they don't really believe they can change.

Research suggests that hope plays a major role in improvements that take place during treatment (Hubble, Duncan, and Miller, 1999). A lack of enthusiasm for treatment that is due to a darkly pessimistic view of the prospects for change is sometimes mistaken for resistance. It's not necessarily that hopeless clients wouldn't want to change; it may be that they see no realistic basis for hope that their efforts will lead to the types of changes they want. Many have tried repeatedly to address the problems in their lives, but have now given up.

Clients rarely present at the first sign of a problem. They more often present when they've lost hope that they can solve the problem on their own (Jerome Frank, cited in Hubble, Duncan, and Miller, 1999). When initial treatment attempts fail to achieve the desired results, clients may lose hope that they can ever solve their problems.

The following techniques are designed to reintroduce hope.

Chapter 1

Hope-Inspiring Reflections

Many hopeless clients make statements that exclude or preclude the possibility of change. "I never do anything right," or "I'm too old to change," or "I was born this way; it's in my genes." But directly challenging this point of view rarely works.

Depressed clients have already been told many times that things aren't so bad. Anorexics have already been told many times that they are not overweight. So far, this has been of little help to them. Worse yet, disagreeing with our clients may make them feel as if we're not listening—that we don't truly understand how much their problems are upsetting them.

Hope-inspiring reflections* offer an alternative to explaining to hopeless clients that "things aren't so bad." They open up possibilities for our clients, while helping them to feel understood.

For example, if a client says "I never do anything right," you might say, "You're feeling like you don't succeed very often." This reflection, which sounds to the untrained ear to be just about the same as what the client said, actually opens up several possibilities.

First, there is the possibility that this idea is only a perception or feeling and may not square with reality. Second, there is the recognition that the client does succeed at least sometimes. Not succeeding very often is infinitely better than never doing anything right. Not succeeding very often is a much more hopeful situation, because you are succeeding to some degree at least some of the time. There is the hope that these exception times can become more frequent with practice.

---

*This section on hope-inspiring reflections is an extension of ideas originally presented by Miller and Rollnick (1991) in *Motivational Interviewing,* and Bill O'Hanlon (Bertolino and O'Hanlon, 1999) in *Invitation to Possibility-Land.*

Your hope-inspiring reflections are designed to offer your client a way of looking at things as less catastrophic. At the same time, you demonstrate your ability to understand and respect the client's point of view. Your reflections help your clients learn to redefine their problems in more accurate, realistic, and solvable ways.

For another example, a client says, "I'm terrible in relationships; women can't stand me, and I always make a fool of myself." You might say, "In the past, your relationships with women haven't worked out as well as you would have liked them to."

This introduces the idea that the problem is "in the past," and not necessarily forever into the future; and, again, the possibility that even though the relationships haven't worked out as well as the client would have liked, they did work out to some small degree—and that's a starting point to build upon.

Other hope-inspiring reflections recognize clients' efforts to overcome the problem. For example, if a client says, "I'll never be happy," you might say, "The way you look at it now, you'll be struggling with these sad feelings a long time." "The way you look at it now" opens up the possibility of a different way to view the problem. The phrase "for a long time" opens up the possibility of an eventual end to the problem.

And this hope-inspiring reflection also acknowledges and encourages action on the part of the client. The "struggling against" suggests that the client is not taking this lying down. It reinforces the idea that the client's choices make a real difference. The client begins to realize that the problem could be even worse if he or she gave up entirely, and that the client can decide to do other things that will have a definite impact on solving the problem. Encouraging and acknowledging action helps clients take an active, rather than passive, approach to therapy.

Still another helpful type of reflection externalizes the problem (Freedman and Combs, 1996; Friedman, 1993; Hopps and Pinderhughes, 1999; Metcalf, 1998; O'Connell, 1998; White and Epston, 1990). For example, a client says, "I'm a fat pig." You might say, "You're feeling as if a weight problem has been getting the best of you lately." The "you're feeling" and "lately" open up the possibilities that this is only a perception, and that it doesn't necessarily have to last forever. Also, the choice of the words "weight problem" separates the problem from the person, in a way that "I'm a fat pig" does not. This helps clients realize that they are not the problem. The problem is the problem, and not an intrinsic and inseparable part of themselves.

People who *have* problems have hope that they can solve them. People who *are* problems, or see themselves as fundamentally and permanently flawed, are less likely to change. Fat pigs cannot realistically hope to live their lives as anything but pigs. There can be no realistic hope that a pig will turn into a gazelle or a zebra. But a person with a weight problem does have a realistic basis for hope that the problem may be successfully addressed.

FIVE TYPES OF HOPE-INSPIRING REFLECTIONS

We have touched on five ways you can reflect back to your hopeless clients that expand their possibilities. They work subtly, but powerfully.

1. *Put the problem in the past, or the solution in the future.* Preface your reflection with "up until now," "recently," "so far," "in the past," "lately," "for a long time," or "at this point," or end it with "yet" (as in "You haven't been able to find a way to keep from drinking yet"). This opens up the possibility that the future will be different.

2. *Introduce the idea that perceptions can be different from reality.* In these cases, your reflection might begin with, "It's your feeling that . . . ," "So in the way you see things . . . ," "It seems as if . . . ," "Your perception is . . . ," and phrases like that. This opens up the possibility that there are other, less pessimistic ways to view the client's situation.

3. *Open up the possibility of exceptions to the problem, especially when clients use exaggerations such as "never" or "always."* If the client says, "I never have any fun," you might reflect, "So there's not as much fun in your life as you would like." Here phrases such as "sometimes," "most of the time," "much of the time," "very often," "not as often as you would like," "less successful than you would like," and "not as satisfying as you would hope" are helpful. They open up the possibility that the client can learn from these exceptions and make them happen more often.

4. *Acknowledge, expect, anticipate, and encourage action on the part of the client.* Here use phrases such as "battling against," "grappling with," "struggling with," "trying to overcome," or "doing your

best." This opens up the possibility that clients can address problems, rather than passively and powerlessly watch their own lives as if they were spectators and not participants.

5. *Externalize the problem.* These reflections can often be combined with the acknowledging/expecting action type when you say, "So you've been fighting these sad feelings . . . ," "Your struggle with the green-eyed monster . . . ," or "These times when [problem] gets the best of you. . . ." This opens up possibilities for overcoming problems, rather than maintaining the status quo. This technique can be especially helpful with children, who often blame themselves for things that are beyond their control.

It's very important to fight our urge to disagree with a hopeless statement, and we sometimes have to go against our first instincts. Don't tell someone with an eating disorder, for example, that you think they are very attractive, and not fat at all. They've been told this many times by many people, and it hasn't helped. It's the same with "Cheer up, things aren't so bad" to somebody who's depressed. It just doesn't work.

Even worse, as already noted, this type of cheerleading may cause your clients to feel as if you are not really listening, nor fully appreciating what they are going through. So resist the urge to tell your clients that things aren't so bad. Hope-inspiring reflections will make your clients feel heard and open up a wide range of possibilities for them. Once clients are more open to these possibilities, other techniques have a better chance to be successful.

HOPE-INSPIRING REFLECTIONS: PRACTICE AND RESPONSES

Consider each of the following client statements. Then take a moment to design a hope-inspiring reflection. It may be helpful to use a pen and paper to write down each client statement, your possible response, and which of the five types of hope-inspiring reflections you are using (putting problems in the past; perceptions differ from reality; acknowledging exceptions; encouraging action; externalization).

We've offered two possible responses for each client statement at the end of this chapter, so that you may compare them to your own. (We list just two of many possibly helpful responses to each client statement.)

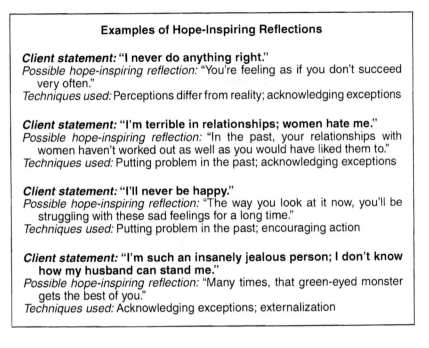

Examples of Hope-Inspiring Reflections

Client statement: "I never do anything right."
Possible hope-inspiring reflection: "You're feeling as if you don't succeed very often."
Techniques used: Perceptions differ from reality; acknowledging exceptions

Client statement: "I'm terrible in relationships; women hate me."
Possible hope-inspiring reflection: "In the past, your relationships with women haven't worked out as well as you would have liked them to."
Techniques used: Putting problem in the past; acknowledging exceptions

Client statement: "I'll never be happy."
Possible hope-inspiring reflection: "The way you look at it now, you'll be struggling with these sad feelings for a long time."
Techniques used: Putting problem in the past; encouraging action

Client statement: "I'm such an insanely jealous person; I don't know how my husband can stand me."
Possible hope-inspiring reflection: "Many times, that green-eyed monster gets the best of you."
Techniques used: Acknowledging exceptions; externalization

Client statement: **"I'm a terrible mother."**
Possible hope-inspiring reflection:

Techniques used:

Client statement: **"I never finish anything I start," or "I'll always be a quitter."**
Possible hope-inspiring reflection:

Techniques used:

Client statement: **"I'll always be a fat pig."**
Possible hope-inspiring reflection:

Techniques used:

Client statement: **"I'm too old to change."**
Possible hope-inspiring reflection:

Techniques used:

Client statement: **"My life is a mess."**
Possible hope-inspiring reflection:

Techniques used:

Client statement: **"Nobody loves me."**
Possible hope-inspiring reflection:

Techniques used:

Client statement: **"I'll never quit smoking."**
Possible hope-inspiring reflection:

Techniques used:

Client statement: **"I'm an addict. I was born that way."**
Possible hope-inspiring reflection:

Techniques used:

Client statement: **"I'm a bad boy, because I get mad at my mommy and don't listen to her."**
Possible hope-inspiring reflection:

Techniques used:

Client statement: **"I wish I were dead."**
Possible hope-inspiring reflection:

Techniques used:

* * *

Client statement: "I'm a terrible mother."
Possible hope-inspiring reflection: "You're feeling like you're not as good a mom as you would like to be."
Techniques used: Perceptions differ from reality; acknowledging exceptions
Alternate possibility for hope-inspiring reflection: "You'd like to find ways to be a better mom than you have been lately."
Techniques used: Encouraging action; putting problem in the past

Client statement: "I never finish anything I start" or "I'll always be a quitter."
Possible hope-inspiring reflection: "Your perception is that you don't follow through on things as often or as well as you'd like to."
Techniques used: Perceptions differ from reality; encouraging action; acknowledging exceptions
Alternate possibility for hope-inspiring reflection: "The temptation to give up gets the best of you sometimes."
Techniques used: Externalization, acknowledging exceptions

Client statement: "I'll always be a fat pig."
Possible hope-inspiring reflection: "It seems to you as if you'll be struggling with a weight problem for a long time."
Techniques used: Perceptions differ from reality; encouraging action; externalization; putting problem in the past
Alternate possibility for hope-inspiring reflection: "Your many attempts to lose weight have not been as successful as you might have liked."
Techniques used: Encouraging action, acknowledging exceptions

Client statement: "I'm too old to change."
Possible hope-inspiring reflection: "The way you see it, it's very difficult for people your age who are trying to change."
Techniques used: Perceptions differ from reality; acknowledging exceptions; encouraging action
Alternate possibility for hope-inspiring reflection: "Until now, you've always felt that changing is difficult as we get older."
Techniques used: Putting problem in the past, perceptions differ from reality

Client statement: "My life is a mess."
Possible hope-inspiring reflection: "You're feeling as if there are a lot of problems in your life you'd like to address."
Techniques used: Perceptions differ from reality; encouraging action
Alternate possibility for hope-inspiring reflection: "So far your attempts to straighten out your life haven't met with much success."
Techniques used: Putting problem in the past, encouraging action, acknowledging exceptions

Client statement: "Nobody loves me."
Possible hope-inspiring reflection: "You're feeling like people don't care about you as much as you'd like them to."
Techniques used: Perceptions differ from reality; acknowledging exceptions
Alternate possibility for hope-inspiring reflection: "So far, you haven't been able to develop as many friendships as you would like."
Techniques used: Putting problem in the past, encouraging action, acknowledging exceptions

Client statement: "I'll never quit smoking."
Possible hope-inspiring reflection: "The way you're feeling now, quitting cigarettes is going to be very difficult for you."
Techniques used: Perceptions differ from reality; encouraging action; putting problem in the past
Alternate possibility for hope-inspiring reflection: "Smoking cigarettes is a habit that you expect will be very difficult to break."
Techniques used: Externalization, encouraging action

Client statement: "I'm an addict; I was born that way."
Possible hope-inspiring reflection: "From your point of view, it's very difficult for some people to change, because of their genes."
Techniques used: Perceptions differ from reality; acknowledging exceptions
Alternate possibility for hope-inspiring reflection: "You're feeling as if your genes are making it more difficult for you to maintain a sober lifestyle."
Techniques used: Perceptions differ from reality, encouraging action

***Client statement:* "I'm a bad boy because I get mad at my mommy and don't listen to her."**
Possible hope-inspiring reflection: "So sometimes you get a visit from 'Mr. Grumpy,' and he makes you do things you'd rather not—like disobey your mom."
Techniques used: Acknowledging exceptions; externalization
Alternate possibility for hope-inspiring reflection: "You feel disappointed in yourself for those times when you don't mind your mom."
Techniques used: Perceptions differ from reality, acknowledging exceptions

***Client statement:* "I wish I were dead."**
Possible hope-inspiring reflection: "Sometimes you feel like life isn't worth the trouble." (This reflection assumes that a suicide assessment has determined that there is no indication for additional precautions regarding possible suicide.)
Techniques used: Acknowledging exceptions
Alternate possibility for hope-inspiring reflection: "At this point in your life, you're struggling to find reasons to go on, or ways to make your life meaningful."
Techniques used: Putting problem in the past, encouraging action

Chapter 2

Scaling

Scaling is a technique (Berg, 1994; Berg and Miller, 1992; Berg and Reuss, 1998; Cade and O'Hanlon, 1993; Hudson, 1996; Friedman, 1993; Littrell, 1998; McFarland, 1995; Metcalf, 1998; Miller, Hubble, and Duncan, 1996; O'Connell, 1998) that works like this: You ask the client to rate the problem on a scale of one to ten, with one being the absolute *worst* the problem could be, and with ten the absolute best—so good it's not even a problem anymore.

Some really hopeless people might answer "negative ten," and that's okay; they've given you a starting point from which to build hope and measure success. Open possibilities and focus on the future by asking, "What would it mean to be at ten?" This gets the client to consider life without the problem. And it gives you specific long-term goals to strive for.

If clients pick a positive number other than one, it is sometimes helpful to ask them what the difference is between one and the number they chose. This may help hopeless clients identify personal and/or environmental resources helpful to solving the problem. It may also help clients begin to overcome their hopelessness, since they have more basis for hope than persons rating themselves a one. Clients' answers to this question about the difference between where they are and a one is often helpful to counselors, because it helps us understand what the client considers to be meaningful change.

If a client rates the present situation as a three, you might say, "Congratulations, you're thirty percent of the way home!" Whatever number the client gives, ask what it would take to make it just one half of a point higher. You're looking for the absolute *smallest* change that the client would consider a step in the right direction. If your client said negative ten, ask what would make it a negative nine and a half. "What would you have to see happen?"

This is how the scaling technique may help hopeless clients define goals. Make sure the changes are small, specific, and within the client's control. Scaling helps subdivide big goals into relatively easy smaller steps. It helps prevent the client from thinking in black and white ("everything's hopeless" or "everything's fine"), and shows there is a wide range of possibilities besides the present situation.

Scaling helps motivate hopeless clients by proving they can change. Scaling also helps clarify clients' vague complaints (Littrell, 1998). Since we solicit the client's opinion on what type of change is both possible and meaningful, there can be no disagreement on the achievement of progress. This technique helps keep the ball of change rolling (by letting clients see how far they've come) and provides both client and counselor a way to assess continuing progress.

CASE STUDY: WORKPLACE WALLFLOWER

Tanya was nearing the end of the residential phase of her treatment. She was living in a halfway house and had a full-time job. The self-confidence that she had developed in residential treatment seemed to evaporate now that she was in the "real world." She reported feeling out of place at work, and very anxious about not fitting in. Tanya said she was too anxious to even speak with co-workers, unless they asked her a direct question.

GROUP LEADER: On a scale of one to ten, with one being the absolute worst your anxiety at work could be, and ten being so good it wasn't even a problem anymore, where would you say you stand now?

TANYA: Two or three.

GROUP LEADER: And for you to be able to report to the group next time that it's a three or four, what would have to happen?

TANYA: I don't know. I wouldn't be feeling so much anxiety all the time.

GROUP LEADER: Okay. Could we phrase that in a positive way, something you *do* want instead of something you don't want, so you'll have something you're trying to accomplish instead of something you're trying to avoid? [The group leader is helping Tanya state her goals positively.]

TANYA: I'd like to feel comfortable, with a sense of inner peace.

GROUP LEADER: Very good. Now what would be one small step toward this inner peace? It sounds like being more comfortable at work would be a step in the right direction.

TANYA: Yes, I'd really like that.

GROUP LEADER: How would you know you were more comfortable at work? [The group leader is helping Tanya define tasks that she would consider signs of meaningful improvement.]

TANYA: I would talk more to my co-workers, or maybe even ask someone to join me for lunch. I might talk to my supervisor about a problem that's been bothering me. I feel like a freak now. Even when people try to talk to me, I never give more than one-word answers.

GROUP LEADER: If you did talk about the problem with your supervisor, where would that put you on the scale?

TANYA: Way up there! Maybe eight and a half.

GROUP LEADER: And if you had lunch out with a co-worker?

TANYA: Maybe six or seven.

GROUP LEADER: So those would be *really* big accomplishments. Would you rate yourself as a three or four if you spoke with co-workers between now and next session?

TANYA: I speak with co-workers now, but it's only about work. I want to speak about something else, and maybe have a real conversation like a normal person.

GROUP LEADER: Is there someone at work who you think might be easier than the others to talk to?

TANYA: Yes, maybe Frank.

GROUP LEADER: And what might you say to Frank?

TANYA: I've been wanting to ask him to buy cookies my daughter is selling.

GROUP LEADER: Is that something you're confident you could do before our next session?

TANYA: Yes, I think so. I was going to try to do it anyway.

GROUP LEADER: And who is the second easiest person to talk to in your office?

TANYA: I guess Judith.

GROUP LEADER: Can you think of any non-work-related topic of discussion to bring up with her?

TANYA: She's had a cold. I could ask her if she's feeling better.

GROUP LEADER: And if you were able to do both of these things, you could tell us next week you've progressed to a three or four on the scale?

TANYA: Yes.

GROUP LEADER: Would it matter if Frank buys the cookies? [The group leader tries to anticipate any problems in carrying out the task.]

TANYA: [Laughing] No. I'd be disappointed in him, but I'd just be happy that I had enough courage to talk with him about something besides work.

Tanya's plan to speak with two co-workers about nonwork topics would still leave her a long way from the "inner peace" she discussed in group. But the scaling technique may have helped convince Tanya that inner peace was not an impossible dream. There were some small steps that she could take, right away, toward that long-term goal.

ADDITIONAL USES FOR THE SCALING TECHNIQUE

Scaling questions are helpful, not just for chemical dependence problems, but for any factors (such as anger, depression, stress, anxiety, eating disorders, and sexual abuse issues) that the client feels contribute to the chemical dependence. Scaling questions can also help clients identify supportive relationships and hidden strengths (Berg, 1994). Ask clients how others might rate them on the same question that they are rating themselves. This will often reveal that some of their helping relationships have more confidence in them than they do in themselves.

As with all scaling questions, it is the follow-up questions, identifying doable tasks that are meaningful to the client, that make the technique effective. Once the client has identified others who rate them higher, you might ask questions such as, "Why does your wife rate you higher than you rate yourself?," "What would she say is the difference between how she looks at your situation and how you look at it?," "Do you agree with your wife that you are the kind of person who never gives up trying?," and "What do you think your wife would say you'd have to do to move up one point on the scale?"

Counselors have also found it helpful to scale the solution, level of hopefulness, and level of confidence, and to use scaling as a means of assessing continuing progress (Berg and Reuss, 1998).

When scaling solutions, your question might be: "On a scale of one to ten, with one meaning you have no idea of how to proceed, and ten meaning you know exactly what you need to do to solve this problem, where would you place yourself now?"

When scaling hopefulness, you might say: "On a scale of one to ten, with ten meaning that you are very optimistic and confident that you will change, and one meaning that you see no chance of changing, where would you rate yourself now?"

When scaling confidence, you might say, "On a scale of one to ten, with one meaning that you have no confidence you can change, and ten meaning you are sure you can change almost immediately, how would you rate yourself today?"

For hopeless clients with multiple problems, scaling can be used to determine which is most troubling to the client, and so create a hierarchy or order in which to address the problems.

Many other types of scales—besides one to ten—have been used successfully by practitioners. Clients can scale the weight of their problem (O'Connell, 1998), or use colors (dark to bright), colored belts (as in karate), the solar system (distance from the sun), or road map scaling (how close are you to the top of the mountain?) (Littrell, 1998).

Managed care companies have been reported to prefer the concrete numbers of a scaling system to vague assurances that the client is on track, especially when requesting additional treatment visits. Some have even accepted therapist scales as the treatment goal (Berg and Reuss, 1998).

CASE STUDY: TIPPING THE SCALES

Amanda considered her situation hopeless. She was of the opinion that she had done so many bad things in her life that she could never make up for them. Without seeing the possibility of ever making up for her past mistakes, Amanda had decided to give up on herself. During a group therapy session, group members took turns trying to change her mind—to no avail. The following exchange took place as that group continued. The observations in brackets were not shared with Amanda or the group.

AMANDA: I've done *really* bad things, and *a lot* of them. They're the kinds of things you just can't make up for. [Amanda is stating the problem as she sees it.]

LISA: You haven't done any worse things than most of us. We think we can change.

MARILYN: That's right; we've all done bad things. What makes you think you've done any worse? [Rather than empathizing with Amanda, the group members are challenging Amanda's view of her situation.]

AMANDA: Nobody here knows *all* the things I've done. Some things can't be undone; it's too late to go back and fix them. [The group members' well-meaning attempts to change Amanda's mind may have made her feel as though they're not really listening.]

GROUP LEADER: How many points do you think you are behind?

AMANDA: Points?

GROUP LEADER: Yes, points. We need some way to measure the deficit of bad things you've done. Are you behind fifty points? One hundred? [Rather than create resistance by arguing with Amanda's point of view, the group leader shows genuine interest in Amanda's opinion, and solicits her estimate of just how big a hole she feels she is in.]

AMANDA: Ten thousand points.

GROUP LEADER: Ten thousand points. And if you did a really good thing, like graduate our program, how many points would that be worth? Five hundred? [Again, the group leader shows respect for Amanda's opinion by accepting her estimate of 10,000 points.]

AMANDA: Yes, five hundred is about right.

GROUP LEADER: And if you did a really small thing, like take the time to talk to someone who feels down, or pick up a gum wrapper from the street and put in it in the garbage?

AMANDA: Ten points.

GROUP LEADER: And if you kept track of all such things, would you ever be able to make up ten thousand points?

AMANDA: Yes, I would.

Amanda agreed to set up a balance sheet with a beginning entry of -10,000 points, and keep track of her good deeds until she was in the black. This creative use of the scaling technique helped Amanda see possibilities she hadn't seen before.

Chapter 3

Normalizing and Reframing

Normalizing and reframing techniques (Berg, 1994; Cade and O'Hanlon, 1993; Eron and Lund, 1996; Fisch and Schlanger, 1999; Friedman, 1993; Hubble, Duncan, and Miller, 1999; Miller, Hubble, and Duncan, 1996; O'Connell, 1998; White and Epston, 1990) offer clients a different way to look at the same set of concrete circumstances that brought them to treatment. For the hopeless client, successful reframes bring new meaning to these circumstances and build upon the idea that change is indeed possible.

Reframing has been defined as "a universal therapeutic technique.... Generally, a therapist induced change in perspective which often leads clients to corresponding changes in attitude and behaviors" (Cooper, 1995, pp. 90-91). It has also been defined as giving clients a new frame of reference within their existing belief system (O'Hanlon and Wiener-Davis, 1989). Clients' views are reframed when they see an experience or situation in a new way (Friedman, 1993). Normalizing is the reframing of a client's experience as undesirable, but still within the normal range of human reactions (Fisch and Schlanger, 1999).

The reframing technique—like all others in this text—should be offered gently. You are merely proposing a more accurate (or equally compelling) and more helpful view of the client's situation. If your reframes attempt to beat clients over the head with a "superior" view, win clients over with a less accurate but "nicer" view, or merely encourage them to adopt a more expedient view, you won't end up being very helpful.

In *Narrative Solutions in Brief Therapy,* the authors share a story about how they once mishandled the reframing technique, and take themselves to task for it.

Mistakes like this made us think twice about waving a therapeutic wand and pulling a reframe out of the hat. Simply twisting the meaning of behavior by arbitrarily relabeling craziness as laziness, madness as badness or sadness, or symptoms as assets was not enough. Although we might have wished it were so, frogs could not so easily be turned into princes. (Eron and Lund, 1996, p. 28)

Cade and O'Hanlon (1993) sound a similar warning in *A Brief Guide to Brief Therapy:* "no frame will be of any help unless it makes more than just intellectual sense . . . frames are not pulled out of the air . . . but guided by direct information often painstakingly gained from the client" (p. 114).

NONPROBLEMS

In the course of my work, I've heard literally hundreds of "nonproblems" reported as tragic personality flaws. In contrast to the type of clients we'll deal with in Section II—those said to be in denial that *anything* is wrong with them—hopeless clients often think that *everything* is wrong with them. They pathologize some of our most ordinary, everyday emotions.

A woman once presented this problem to a group therapy session: "I want people to like me." I told her that, luckily, there's a support group for that. It's called *everybody!* Other nonproblems I've heard about firsthand include, "I like pleasure better than pain," "I want to be in control of my own life," "I always want to look my best," and "I enjoy sex too much."

I'm not kidding. People pay thousands upon thousands of dollars to sex therapists because they're not enjoying sex enough, yet other people view satisfying sex as a problem. Many times, of course, there are real problems that are somehow related to the nonproblem the client is distressed about. The woman who said she enjoyed sex too much eventually came to believe that her choice of sexual partners and level of self-esteem were problematic, and that her sexuality was a gift from God which she should treat with more respect.

Hopeless clients often find it hard to believe that they have many of the exact same feelings that others, whom they admire, share. The desire to be loved, for example, is nearly universal. Yet hopeless clients often see their desire to be loved as a sign of how much they are different.

CASE STUDY: TO ERR IS HUMAN

In a group setting, Cassie expressed her hopelessness that she could ever view herself as a person of value. Her written group preparation, which she read in group before a discussion, contained the self-judgment, "I've denied and rejected my humanity." The group leader was troubled by the heavy burden Cassie had placed on herself.

GROUP LEADER: You said in your written prep that you "denied and rejected your humanity." Can you tell me more about that?

CASSIE: I've never lived up to my full potential as a human being. I've disappointed my Creator, by accepting less for myself and never accomplishing anything.

GROUP LEADER: You're feeling as if God doesn't love you very much?

CASSIE: How could He?

GROUP LEADER: Isn't that His job? [There is an awkward silence as Cassie looks disapprovingly at the group leader, perhaps for what she saw as an inappropriate or insensitive attempt at humor. The group leader realizes he is in over his head in discussing theology, and returns to his original question.]

GROUP LEADER: As far as specific things you've done, which ones contributed to your observation that you have denied and rejected your humanity?

CASSIE: I don't know . . . everything. I never finish anything I start; I've spent thousands of dollars of my parents' money at six different schools that I never finished. I'm old enough to where I should have amounted to something, and I haven't.

GROUP LEADER: Having denied and rejected your humanity, do you feel it's too late to get it back?

CASSIE: I don't know.

GROUP LEADER: Could we consider an alternate explanation for your dropping out of school so many times?

CASSIE: Like what?

GROUP LEADER: Could we simply say that you've made some mistakes?

CASSIE: It's more than that.

GROUP LEADER: Can we say that you've made some very big mistakes, and some of the same ones many times?

CASSIE: Yes.

GROUP LEADER: And could we say that by making mistakes, you have confirmed your humanity—rather than denied it? It seems to me that humans make mistakes all the time. You would be nonhuman if you didn't make mistakes.

The group leader has presented the case for Cassie's "denial and rejection of her humanity" as a nonproblem. His feeling was that Cassie had several real and pressing problems that needed to be addressed, and that this "denial and rejection of her humanity" idea was only getting in her way.

Rather than reframing, the group leader chose to address what he considered to be a nonproblem by *deframing*. The technique of deframing (Cade and O'Hanlon, 1993) challenges the self-defeating view of the client, without offering an alternative. This allows clients the option of rejecting the deframing, accepting the deframing, discovering alternate meanings for themselves, or deciding there may be no particular meaning at all.

NORMALIZING TECHNIQUES

Normalizing (also called universalizing) techniques (Berg, 1994; Metcalf, 1998; O'Hanlon and Weiner-Davis, 1989) can help hopeless clients realize that things aren't as bad as they think they are. They can be used to introduce doubt to clients' inaccurate beliefs that are obstacles to their recoveries.

You can normalize your clients' situations through what you say, and by what you don't say (O'Hanlon and Weiner-Davis, 1989). This can be done by letting your clients know that you are familiar with the types of problems they are presenting, and that many have overcome similar situations.

You can help to normalize through what you don't say by refraining from gasping, offering condolences, or applying labels. Hopeless clients often benefit from our spoken and unspoken assurances that their difficulties are solvable ones. In other words, help clients understand that it is normal to have problems.

As Hayes, Strosahl, and Wilson (1999) put it,

> short of giving nearly every citizen one or more syndromal labels, no amount of progress in the area of psychological disease will remove our need to explain and address the pervasiveness of human suffering. *Most* humans are hurting—just some more than others. It is, in effect, normal to be abnormal. (italics in original, p. 8)

And as Duncan and Miller observe in *The Heroic Client,* "once a label has been attached, it sticks like glue. The diagnosed person accepts the identity implied by the label and develops the expected role and outlook. Unnecessary and crippling hopelessness may result" (Duncan and Miller, 2000, p. 49).

Many hopeless clients are hopeless, in part, because they've labeled themselves, or accepted labels. They feel permanently flawed and unchangeable. Most labels are not helpful, because they define the person as the problem, and limit and end the person with the problem. They don't include those possibilities we talked about earlier. Reframing techniques help hopeless clients look at the same old problems in brand-new ways.

We might encourage a client to restate a problem in a more solvable way than by applying a label. This is often helpful, whether the label is professional jargon or not. If a client says, "I'm a nervous wreck," for example, you might ask, "What's the difference between a nervous wreck and a person who worries more than they want to?" "Worrying less" just seems like a much easier thing to do than dealing with a "nervous wreck."

This formula for normalizing or reframing is offered in *In Search of Solutions* (O'Hanlon and Weiner-Davis, 1989). The authors suggest asking a question such as, "How can you tell the difference between X [the hopeless client's exaggerated view of the problem] and Y [a normalized explanation for it]?" In their example, the parents of a teenager have diagnosed their daughter with depression, and they are asked how they can tell the difference between depression and typical teenage moodiness.

DSM (Diagnostic and Statistical Manual of Mental Disorders) diagnoses are useful on insurance forms and in conversations among professionals, but they do not seem to be very helpful to hopeless clients, who often do not meet the diagnostic criteria for the disorder they have hung on themselves. We can be helpful to these clients by helping them reframe their problems in a less pathological way. The following offers a list of self-diagnoses that were later traded in for more accurate and specific descriptions.

Reframing Problems for Hopeless Clients

The left column includes hopeless clients' self-diagnoses. When asked to describe the basis for the diagnoses, the result was the discovery of a problem that sounded much easier to solve than the "disorder" they first used to describe themselves. Although the two columns include alternative descriptions of the same symptom, the ones on the right are more likely to inspire hope because they sound easier to solve.

Less hopeful problem description	*More hopeful problem description*
• I'm obsessive-compulsive.	• I wash my hands more times a day than I would like.
• I'm codependent.	• The ways I've been trying to be helpful to my spouse haven't been working very well.
• I have an anxiety disorder.	• My mouth gets dry when I have to speak before large groups.

REFRAMING CLIENT PROBLEMS:
PRACTICE AND RESPONSES

Consider the following self-diagnoses and think about how you might respond. Some possible reframes are offered at the end of this chapter. Remember that DSM diagnoses mean a very specific set of circumstances to a clinician. But those same labels could mean a great number of very different things to hopeless clients. Possible responses are suggested on the next page.

If a hopeless client says: **"I'm totally neurotic."**
You might say:

If a hopeless client says: **"I'm passive-aggressive."**
You might say:

If a hopeless client says: **"I'm a narcissist."**
You might say:

If a hopeless client says: **"I'm manic-depressive."**
You might say:

* * *

If a hopeless client says: "I'm totally neurotic."
You might say: "So some of the things you worry about aren't really that important?"

If a hopeless client says: "I'm passive-aggressive."
You might say: "Do you mean you don't like feeling obligated to do certain things, and react strongly when certain expectations are placed upon you?" or "Are you saying that you can be spiteful sometimes?"

If a hopeless client says: "I'm a narcissist."
You might say: "Are you saying you desperately want people to love and admire you?"

If a client says: "I'm manic-depressive."
You might say: "Do you mean that you don't always have as much control over your moods as you would like?"

CASE STUDY: PROGRESS IN DISGUISE

One afternoon I was called from my office for an "emergency" counseling session with a client who was talking about leaving our treatment program against clinical advice. Susan was feeling especially hopeless that day, despite some very exciting changes she had made during the first few weeks of her stay.

SUSAN: I'm the same old Susan. I thought I was changing, but now I feel like leaving and getting high. [Susan was visibly upset, on the verge of tears.]

COUNSELOR: The same old Susan?

SUSAN: It's not working. I split from three other programs to get high, and now I feel like doing it again. [Susan was painting her situation as hopeless.]

COUNSELOR: Wouldn't the same old Susan have been gone already? [The therapist is aware of progress that Susan has made, which he tries to get her in touch with.]

SUSAN: What do you mean?

COUNSELOR: You're still here, and you asked to speak to a counselor. What else do you notice as different this time?

SUSAN: Nothing's different. Once a junkie, always a junkie. Nobody thought I could do it, and they were right. [The therapist's initial attempts to get Susan in touch with her progress are less than successful; Susan may be too upset to think clearly.]

COUNSELOR: It seems to upset you very much, these cravings and this desire to leave treatment.

SUSAN: Of course it upsets me, you asshole. [Susan is openly hostile; perhaps she has mistaken the therapist's tone for sarcasm, or is upset the therapist is so out of touch with her feelings that he has to ask, while she's crying nearly hysterically, if she's upset.]

COUNSELOR: It upsets you more than it ever did before?

SUSAN: Yes! [Susan's tone of voice says "leave me alone."]

COUNSELOR: That's very good!

[Already near the end of her rope, Susan glares at the therapist. She appears too angry to even speak.]

COUNSELOR: Are you saying that you care, more than you ever have before, about being able to maintain sobriety? [The therapist again tries to help Susan connect with the progress she has made in treatment.]

SUSAN: I guess I do. [Susan's tone seems to imply she feels the therapist has asked another stupid question, one he should have already known the answer to.]

COUNSELOR: And instead of giving in to your cravings and leaving, like the old Susan would have done, the new Susan sought out her counselor.

SUSAN: [This observation seems to stop Susan in her tracks.] Yeah. [Spoken more to communicate the idea of "I'm listening" than to signal agreement.]

COUNSELOR: Well, congratulations.

[Susan still looks skeptical, but no longer hostile.]

COUNSELOR: I think you may look back on this as a very important day in your life. Not only have you triumphed over the same kinds of cravings that got the best of you before, but you seem to care more about yourself than you ever have before. I'm really proud of the changes you've made.

SUSAN: [Susan sits and thinks for a long while before speaking again. She seems to be unsure if she has really made progress, or is being tricked into thinking so.] Do you really think I'm different, or are you just saying that?

COUNSELOR: [Looking Susan directly in the eyes] I really think you're different.

SUSAN: Maybe I am.

Rather than being a cause for disappointment, Susan's situation was a cause for celebration. But without the therapist to reframe it for her, she might have gotten discouraged and given up.

Chapter 4

Exploring Exceptions

We can often learn more from the one time we do things right than from the hundreds of times we do things wrong. Hopeless clients sometimes assume that they've survived only by "luck," and they may not realize all they are doing to keep the problem from getting worse. They may dismiss times without the problem as random aberrations outside their control. We can develop a close relationship with our clients just as easily by discussing their strengths and possible solutions to their problems as we can by discussing their shortcomings and possible explanations for the problems.

A favorite technique of solution-focused therapists, exploring exceptions, helps clients get in touch with "hidden" strengths (Berg and Miller, 1992; Berg and Reuss, 1998; Cade and O'Hanlon, 1993; Hudson, 1996; McFarland, 1995: Metcalf, 1998; Miller, Hubble, and Duncan, 1996; Miller and Berg, 1995; O'Connell, 1998; O'Hanlon and Weiner-Davis, 1989). Narrative therapists call these exceptions "unique outcomes" or "sparkling moments," which contradict "problem-saturated stories," and they see them as doorways to better outcomes (Freedman and Combs, 1996). The idea is to identify personal and environmental resources that are at the client's disposal, so they may be deployed to combat the problem. Once exceptions have been identified, we can work with clients to encourage more of what is already working for them and help them transfer competence we have found in other areas to impact the problem. Exceptions may include an especially helpful way of viewing a situation or an underused way of doing something that is more successful than the usual way.

Try talking to your clients about the times they were sober, or when whatever problem you are addressing was not as bad. What was different about those days? What were they thinking differently? Feeling differently? Doing differently?

Clients are often able to identify a set of things—thoughts, feelings, and patterns of behavior over which they have control—that gets them more satisfying results. When they look at life in these specific ways, and have these specific feelings, and do these specific things, they are much more likely to be happy with the outcome.

For example, with hopeless clients who are depressed, the first response to exploring exceptions is often, "I'm always depressed," or "I'm never happy." But explore a little further, and you'll find out about times they were slightly less depressed than others—perhaps times they got out of bed sooner or had more social contact. Ask about what they did differently and what others would say they noticed that was different on those days. Help clients identify whatever environmental or personal resources were helpful during these exception times, and encourage them to help the exception times happen more often.

CASE STUDY: EXCEPTIONAL DAY

Sarah saw herself as a hopeless alcoholic. She had been through several programs, graduating them all and relapsing soon thereafter.

SARAH: Outside of residential treatment, I've never been able to stop drinking. I've been through eleven short- and long-term programs, but they didn't help. I've never been able to stop drinking until I pass out.

GROUP LEADER: So you feel as if there have been very few times you've been able to stay sober outside of treatment. [The therapist tries a hope-inspiring reflection. His hope is that he will be able to show Sarah that her perception of herself may be too harsh, and that there have been exceptions to the problem.]

SARAH: Not a "very few times." *Never.* In over three years, there's been only one day [outside of treatment] where I stopped drinking before I passed out. [Later on in treatment, Sarah realized this was not an accurate statement, but for now this was her perception.]

GROUP LEADER: So you were successful at limiting your drinking on one day. How did you manage to do that? [The therapist is "encouraging action" and trying to identify coping skills the client may have missed.]

SARAH: Of course I stopped drinking *that* day. My child had an accident and I had to take her to the hospital.

GROUP LEADER: Tell me more about that day.

SARAH: My mom hadn't come downstairs yet. Tiffany had pulled the tablecloth off our dining room table, and the heavy centerpiece smashed her leg. I felt so guilty for not watching her more closely. I raced to the emergency ward, and they took care of her. I felt so bad when I saw her little leg in a cast.

GROUP LEADER: So you handled this emergency without relying on your mom? [The therapist is pointing out an exception to Sarah's usual willingness to let her mother take responsibility for the care of her child.]

SARAH: I didn't have time to think! I just did what any mother would do when her baby girl was hurt.

GROUP LEADER: It sounds like you acted very responsibly. How do you think the emergency room personnel saw you that day? Did they see a hopeless alcoholic?

SARAH: I'm sure *they* didn't see that. They probably see a lot of moms in my situation. They could tell I cared about Tiffany a lot.

GROUP LEADER: On this day, the hospital staff saw you as a concerned mother?

SARAH: I suppose so.

GROUP LEADER: You love your daughter very much, and you can control your drinking when you have a good enough reason.

SARAH: It's weird that you say that, because that was the one night I can remember that I didn't drink—even after I knew Tiffany was home and okay and my mom could have watched her. I was just so guilty for not watching her better I couldn't drink.

The counselor went on to closely examine every aspect of that day with Sarah. She realized she was capable of acting as a responsible parent in a very difficult situation, and it became impossible for her to look at her situation as totally hopeless. Sarah realized that, along with the guilt she felt for not watching Tiffany more closely, she felt good about the way she handled herself the rest of that day.

She realized that Tiffany saw her differently that day as well, and she wanted to be the kind of mom she was on that day more often. Sarah eventually realized that although that exception day was a major emergency, Tiffany's need for a real mom was no less urgent on every other day. She felt she had good reasons to change and, at last, some real hope that change was possible.

In the following exchange, with a different client in a different group, the group leader helps Tina identify specific ways she has dealt successfully with her anger.

TINA: I don't know why I get so mad sometimes. I can't even think straight.

GROUP LEADER: So sometimes you really lose your cool, and sometimes you can keep a lid on your anger pretty well.

TINA: Yeah, I don't know why.

GROUP LEADER: What are you doing differently those times when you handle your anger pretty well?

TINA: I really don't know. [Tina has not considered the possibility that the way she chooses to think and act can make a difference.]

GROUP LEADER: Tell us about the last time you handled your anger pretty well.

TINA: [After thinking a few seconds] It was last week. Kaitlyn told me I didn't clean my room well enough, and that would usually make me fly off the handle.

GROUP LEADER: But this time you didn't? I'm proud of you. Tell us how you managed to keep your cool, and what you did instead of "flying off the handle."

TINA: Well, I talked calmly.

GROUP LEADER: So you find that you get better results when you talk calmly, and what else did you do?

TINA: Well, I gave her a chance to talk.

GROUP LEADER: You took turns talking. And what else?

TINA: I really listened to what she had to say.

GROUP LEADER: And you really listened. That seems to have worked out much better for you. What else did you do differently than the times when you fly off the handle?

TINA: Well, I didn't think, like, "this girl is out to get me" or anything like that.

GROUP LEADER: That's great! So you find that when you give the other person a better chance to talk, stay calm, really listen to what's being said, and keep in mind that the other person isn't "out to get you," you can handle your anger pretty well.

TINA: I guess so.

Hopeless clients often explain away, as accidents or quirks of fate, any times that they handle themselves well in a problematic situation. In this brief exchange, the group leader has succeeded in helping Tina identify at least four specific strategies that have been helpful to her in dealing with her anger in the past. That makes it more likely that Tina will choose to use these same strategies in the future.

TECHNIQUES FOR EXPLORING EXCEPTIONS

For people who only drink or use on weekends, or never drink or use before a certain time of day, ask questions that help get clients in touch with the successful strategies they are employing during those nondrinking or nonusing times. You can uncover exceptions by asking questions, directly observing your client, or sometimes by just listening closely.

Here are some typical opening exception-exploring requests:

- Tell me about the times this problem is just a little bit less severe.
- Tell me about the times this problem was more manageable than you might have expected.
- Tell me about the times when you haven't even had this problem.

And some possible follow-up questions:

- What were you doing differently?
- How did you feel differently?
- What was going on in your mind that was different?
- What would others (family, friends, co-workers, acquaintances, strangers) say was different at those times?
- What happened just before and just after (the exception)?
- Is there a place where this problem is less likely to come up?
- Is there a time of day when this problem is less likely to get the best of you?
- Who is usually around when this (exception) happens?
- What have you learned about yourself that might build your confidence?
- What might you want to do again, the next time this problem comes up?
- Exactly how would you do that?

Many different types of questions may help your clients get in touch with the way they have some influence over their problems. Direct questions such as, "What was the happiest time of your life?," followed up with "What were you doing differently then?" may be helpful.

Likewise, questions about what other people might notice can be beneficial. For example, "What would your husband say is the best thing about the way you handle this problem?"

Exploring exceptions also works well in combination with some techniques we've already discussed, such as scaling and externalizing. For example, you might ask, "What's the closest you've ever been to a ten?" Or you might request, "Tell me more about the times in your day [week, year, life] that you were higher than your current rating." Then follow up by helping to identify details of personal strengths, coping strategies, and environmental factors that your client may take advantage of.

As a follow-up to a hope-inspiring reflection that externalizes the problem, you might request, "Tell me more about those few times you mentioned, when you kept your anger from getting the best of you." Or ask, "What's different on those days when your anxiety is not completely paralyzing?" Or request more information about "that one time you did manage to stop the cravings from overwhelming you."

Hypothetical questions can also be used to explore exceptions. For example, "Suppose your mother was really in trouble, and you had to really keep your cool even though you were very upset. How would you do it?" or "If you did decide you wanted to limit the amount you drink, how would you do it?"

Many times you will notice that what your client is saying contradicts what you are seeing right before your eyes. Clients, during discussions of some of the most intimate and personal details of their lives, have sometimes remarked about their inability to trust people or communicate about sensitive issues. "How are you doing so well communicating now?" I might ask in these situations.

When clients are convinced that they have an insurmountable or uncontrollable problem with their anger, depression, anxiety, ability to reason, communication, level of trust, etc., notice, out loud, the times when your personal experience contradicts their view. And when clients complain about *never* making the right decision, remind them of their decision to seek treatment, and how you admire them for that choice.

When hopeless clients report that there are no exceptions, it is sometimes helpful to ask about what they are doing to keep the problem from becoming even worse. Or you might ask what others would say (spouse, co-workers, family, friends) is different about the times they see an improvement. These additional questions provide additional opportunities for the client to identify hidden strengths.

ADDITIONAL QUESTIONS AND REQUESTS FOR USE IN EXPLORING EXCEPTIONS

- What made you decide to seek treatment?
- Tell me about the times jealousy didn't get the best of you.
- Tell me about the last period of time in your life when you felt things were working out well for you.
- Tell me about the last time your parents felt proud of you.
- When did this first become a problem for you? What was different back then (before the problem started)?
- When are you most likely to avoid this problem?
- How do you make that happen?
- What's the closest you've ever come to solving this problem?
- Who is helpful to you in maintaining your sobriety?
- What are you good at? What are your hobbies and interests?
- What was different during the period of time before your latest relapse?
- How did you solve this problem last time it came up?
- What do you need to do to repeat that success?
- How do you explain those times when you successfully control your drinking? How do you do that?
- Which of those ways that you handle your anger do you consider to be best?
- When is the hurt you carry around the smallest? Are there times when you barely notice it?
- When is this problem least noticeable?
- What's going on in your life that you would like to continue?
- How did you manage to figure that out?
- What made you decide to approach the problem in a different way that day?
- Who's usually around when you're having a good day?
- What are the signs that you're going to handle your jealousy well?
- Which teachers (rules, family members) do you respect?
- So this month has been especially bad. What made things better last month?

- How were you able to overcome the urge to use?
- How have you been coping all this time?
- What have you been doing to keep this problem from getting worse?
- How do you find the strength to face these situations?
- Tell me about the times you aren't angry; resist the urge to drink; get along well with your spouse; really enjoy life; are optimistic you can solve this problem; are glad you're alive; are happy you are not somebody else.

Just as with the reframing technique, it's the follow-up questions that will really make the difference. Be sure follow-up questions connect the exceptions to a solution that is acceptable to the client. Help your clients use what they have learned by exploring exceptions to their maximum advantage.

One word of caution about use of the exploring exceptions technique: It's a mistake to use it so enthusiastically that you don't allow the client to feel "heard." As noted in *The New Language of Change,*

> Our preference is to talk about solutions rather than problems; however, that may not immediately fit with the experience of our clients, who often come to therapy intending or expecting to talk about problems. We do not believe that talking about the problem ("working it through") leads to change; however we are clear that *not* talking about it sometimes leads to clients feeling unheard. Therefore, while our aim is to alert to exceptions to the problem, or other examples of competence from the outset of therapy, we are alert to our clients' lead and to signs that they need to know that their situation has been understood and their experience validated. (Friedman, 1993, p. 110)

Chapter 5

Externalizing Problems

We have already touched upon the idea of externalizing problems in the context of hope-inspiring reflections. This section will more fully explore this technique as an approach that may restore hope to hopeless clients.

One goal of externalization, also called depersonalization, is to help clients "recapture their belief in the possibility of change" (Miller, Hubble, and Duncan, 1997, p. 158). Those problems considered to be inherent in the client are rendered less fixed and less restricting (White and Epston, 1990). "Externalizing conversations can separate a person from internalized shame and guilt and stimulate personal agency, creativity, and choice in a person's relationship with a problem" (Friedman, 1993, p. 189).

Though it's not usually called externalization, the practice is central to many effective therapeutic approaches. Rather than clients themselves being the problem, the problem is attributed to a disease, childhood trauma, brain chemistry, a defective gene, or distorted cognitions (Miller, Hubble, and Duncan, 1997).

When clients are convinced they are the problem, it is much more difficult for them to get in touch with their nonproblem identity. For many hopeless clients, externalizing helps undercut their feelings of personal failure. It helps clients separate themselves from problems that may have been dominating their lives for a long time (White and Epston, 1990). Besides renewed hope in the possibility of a solution to the problem, externalizing also helps eliminate the feeling of blame and the need for defensiveness, while at the same time facilitating accountability for the problem.

Externalizing in no way lets clients "off the hook" of accepting responsibility for their choices. As White and Epston (1990) point out, the exact opposite is true.

> While practices associated with the externalizing of problems enable persons to separate themselves and their relationships from such problems, these practices do not separate persons from responsibility for the extent to which they participate in the survival of the problem. In fact, as these practices help persons become aware of and describe their relationship with the problem, they enable them to assume responsibility for the problem, something they could not do beforehand. (p. 65)

Seeing problems and people as separate allows clients and counselors to enter a collaborative relationship with each other against the problem (Freedman and Combs, 1996). The idea is to portray the problem as one that *bothers* the client, rather than *defines* the client (Metcalf, 1998).

As hypothesized in *Acceptance and Commitment Therapy,*

> For example, a client will say, "I *am* depressed." The statement looks like a description but it is not. It suggests that the client has fused with the verbal label and treated it as a matter of essence or identity, not emotion. "I am depressed" casts a feeling as an issue of being—"am" is, after all, just a form of the word "be." At a descriptive level what is happening is something more like "I am a person who is having a feeling called 'depression' at this moment." (Hayes, Strosahl, and Wilson, 1999, pp. 72-73)

And from *Narrative Therapy,*

> We believe that separating people from problems makes it more likely that they will be able to act responsibly . . .
> When people see themselves as problematic, they often feel helpless to do anything about their plight . . . there is little room to get free of a problem when that problem is oneself.
> When we see ourselves as separate from our problems, we can take responsibility for our relationships with them and decide what to do in relation to them. (Freedman and Combs, 1996, p. 283)

Freedman and Combs (1996) see externalizing as more important as an attitude or approach to treatment than a treatment technique. "It creates a different 'receiving context for people's stories,' one in which we can work to understand their problems without seeing them as problematic or pathological" (p. 50).

In other words, people are not problems and could never be problems. They have relationships with problems. When clients see themselves as the problem, they are less hopeful, less motivated, and less likely to change. And when as counselors we see clients as problems—embodiments of resistance and denial—we aren't in as good a position to be helpful.

TURNING ADJECTIVES INTO NOUNS

One relatively simple way to externalize a problem is to turn it from an adjective into a noun (Freedman and Combs, 1996), as in the example of talking about a client's relationship with feelings of depression rather than a "depressed client." The counselor might explore exceptions by asking a question such as, "When this depression looks like it's about to take over, what kinds of things help keep it away?" rather than continuing a discussion of the depressed client.

Once you and the client are speaking about the problem as if it is separate from the client (either by changing an adjective into a noun, personifying the problem, or having the client give it a name), you can engage the client in a discussion of *how* the problem is a problem. You might ask "How does this [problem] disrupt your life?"

Then you might explore exceptions to the problem and consider any ways the client has successfully dealt with the problem in the past, or kept it from getting worse. If exploring exceptions is productive, these exceptions can be used as models for future behavior and a foundation to build upon.

If attempts to explore exceptions create resistance or disagreement, discuss the client's ideas for new strategies that might be helpful. The following examples include possible client statements, counselor response, and possible topics for continuing the externalizing discussions.

Examples of Externalizing by Turning Adjectives into Nouns

Client: "I'm such an anxious person."
Counselor: "In what ways does this anxiety interfere with your everyday life?"

Continuing discussion could clearly define the practical problems the anxiety is causing, circumstances most likely to create it, and strategies for keeping it away.

Client: "I'm a really angry person. If you catch me on the wrong day, watch out!"
Counselor: "So sometimes your anger takes over and you can't control it, and other times you can keep it at bay?"

Continuing discussion could explore exceptions to identify currently successful anger management skills and ways to amplify them.

Client: "Everybody says I'm anorexic, so I must be."
Counselor: "You think you might have an unhealthy relationship with food?"

EXTERNALIZING BY TURNING ADJECTIVES INTO NOUNS: PRACTICE AND RESPONSES

Take a moment to consider the following client statements, how you might externalize the problem, and what continuing discussion might be beneficial.

Client: "I can't help it; I'm hyperactive."
Counselor:

Continuing discussion

Client: **"I'm very codependent."**
Counselor:

Continuing discussion

Client: **"I'm very shy, especially around people I've just met."**
Counselor:

Continuing discussion

It can also be helpful when counselors choose nouns instead of adjectives. We can consider the possibility that we might generate resistance and denial—rather than wonder what to do about "resistant" clients. Once it is clear that any resistance or denial is apart and separate from our clients, we can join our clients in an attack upon the problem that cannot possibly be mistaken as an attack on the client. Possible responses are suggested on the next page.

* * *

Client: "I can't help it; I'm hyperactive."
Counselor: "Tell me more about this great energy you have."
Continuing discussion could focus on specifically what the client finds troubling about this energy, and the best way to address it.

Client: "I'm very codependent."
Counselor: "Are you saying that this codependence keeps you from being all that you might be without it?"
Continuing discussion might focus on the future and what the client would be like once the codependence was out of the picture. This would hopefully provide a series of long-term goals.

Client: "I'm very shy, especially around people I've just met."
Counselor: "This shyness gets the best of you sometimes, and it's especially problematic in unfamiliar surroundings."
Continuing discussion might center on how the client acts differently once he or she gets to know people better, and a plan to transfer these relationship skills to people being met for the first time.

Chapter 6

Looking Toward the Future and Clarifying Goals

One characteristic shared by many hopeless clients is the tendency to focus on the past. They may be looking backward to identify the underlying cause of their troubles, with the idea that this will lead to the solution of their problems. Or they may be looking backward and reliving their mistakes in an attempt to identify "what went wrong." But a forward-looking strategy is often more helpful.

As noted by Steven Friedman (1993), "hope is fanned by discussion of future options, rather than dampened by explanations of the problem or recitations of past failures" (p. 26). He also writes that "learning to be the person you want to be is quite different—and often less time consuming—than learning why you are the way you are" (p. 88).

It stands to reason that people with a difficult past tend to have a pessimistic view of the future, and that this pessimism might make them less enthusiastic about exerting great efforts to change. A more optimistic view of the future may translate into motivation to deal with current problems and so facilitate a better future.

Development of a realistic vision for a better future is especially helpful to hopeless clients. The vision must be detailed and seen as realistic from the point of view of the client. Clarifying goals is important because goals that are firmly within the client's awareness are more likely to be achieved than a counselor's goals that are not shared with the client.

Hopeless clients either may be unsure of what they really want or don't believe they could ever achieve what they really want. The questions that follow have been helpful in addressing both situations.

They have been designed to focus on *how* things can be different, rather than *why* things are as they are.

- What would you like to have happen in our session today?
- What will be a sign to you that we are making progress toward your goals?
- How will that improve your situation?
- How will you know when you've handled your problem?
- How will you know when you're not angry (bashful, anxious, or whatever) anymore?
- When you've reached your goal, what will that look like? Give me the details on what the difference will be in your everyday life.
- What will you be doing, feeling, and thinking differently?
- Imagine you woke up one morning without this problem. What's the first thing you'd notice that would be different?
- What's the first thing your family will notice that will be different?
- If we were watching a videotape of you a year from now, when all of this is behind you, tell me exactly what you'd be doing?
- What's the first thing you'd have to do to guarantee a better future?
- What will be your favorite topic of discussion when you are communicating better with your spouse?
- Who will be the most surprised when you've been sober a year?
- Share with me what it would be like if you were completely successful in getting your life to where you wanted it to be.
- What new skills might you have to develop?
- How would you be different?
- How would you be handling things differently?
- Who would be the first to notice?
- Who do you think will be most supportive and helpful?
- Exactly how will they be supportive?
- What do you want to be the same in the future?
- What would your support network look like?
- What will you be doing this week to keep the problem from getting worse?
- How will you keep this ball of change rolling in the right direction?
- How will you feel about yourself once you've accomplished this?

These types of questions can help generate conversations that create opportunities for clients to identify more and better future options. The idea is to help clients see their current difficulties as part of a continuing story that has a happy ending.

Even the most pessimistic views of the future can be springboards for discussion of better things ahead. For example, in *Solution Talk* the authors write,

> Even in cases where the only thing a client can see in the future is suicide, the therapist can pursue a positive future vision by building upon the client's suicide fantasy. After having established a good rapport with the client, the therapist might say, for example, "Suppose that after you die you find yourself at the heavenly gates. You are greeted in a respectful manner by an angel who informs you that your case has been reconsidered and that you have been granted a second chance. When you return to earth you find that your problems are gone and that your life is quite satisfactory. How would life be for you then?" (Furman and Aloha, 1992, pp. 102-103)

This example is one of the many variations of the "miracle question" (Berg and Miller, 1992; Berg and Reuss, 1998; Cade and O'Hanlon, 1993; Friedman, 1993; Furman and Aloha, 1992; Littrell, 1998; McFarland, 1995; O'Hanlon and Weiner-Davis, 1989) in which clients are asked to imagine their lives without the problem. Here are some others:

> Suppose when you go to sleep tonight (pause), a miracle happens and the problems that brought you here are solved (pause). But since you are asleep you can't know this miracle has happened until you wake up tomorrow. What will be different tomorrow that will let you know that this miracle has happened and the problem is solved? (Berg and Reuss, 1998, p. 30)

> Let's imagine that a year has gone by and we all meet somewhere in the town, perhaps in a cafeteria down the road. The sun is shining and to our surprise Minna walks in. She tells us that everything is fine in her life. What would you tell us, Minna? (Furman and Aloha, 1992, p. 95)

We have been completely successful in helping you to reach your goal. It is like we have climbed a mountain and have reached the top. In view of how you wanted your life to be, you have achieved it. What do you see around you? What internal picture do you make? What are you saying about yourself? What are others saying? As you look down the mountain to where you first began, what was the very first step you took to begin to get where we are now? What was the second step? (Littrell, 1998, p. 86)

If I had a magic wand and were able to perform magic on your situation, what will be happening that is different from before? (O'Hanlon and Weiner-Davis, 1989, p. 106)

A major benefit of having clients imagine that their problems are solved is that this often generates very helpful information on how they got there. This often results in highly achievable client-generated goals.

It's important that client goals are stated in the positive. Help clients define and achieve what they *do* want, rather than trying to avoid what they don't want. Getting what you do want is really much easier than avoiding what you don't want. For example, if you want to stop sitting in a chair, the only way to do it is to start doing something else (such as standing or sliding off the chair). Focusing on the negative— "I've got to stop sitting"—doesn't help solve the problem as easily as the positive—"I think I'll start standing."

Consider the following client goals, stated negatively:

- Drink less.
- Don't feel so guilty all the time.
- Stop being afraid of my own shadow.
- Avoid blowing up at my husband.
- Make the pain stop.
- Keep from second-guessing myself all the time.

These negative goals are all focused on the past—on the problems (drinking, guilt, fear, anger, pain, and self-doubt). Positively stated goals focus on the future—and on the solutions. They are highly preferable to negative goals because clients can develop pride and a sense of accomplishment for what they *have* done, instead of settling for things they've *avoided* doing as their biggest accomplishments.

But it's not quite as easy as using the opposite of each negative to form a positive goal. It's better to ask the client a direct question such as, "So you don't want to feel that type of anxiety that crushes your chest and makes you short of breath. What is it that you do want?" The ensuing conversation will likely generate a different set of short- and long-term goals for each client.

One client might answer, "I want to get along better with my mom." Another might say, "I want people to respect me." Still another might say, "I want a promotion at work."

CASE STUDY: THE MIRACLE QUESTION

The following case study demonstrates the use of a miracle-type question. Claudia was a woman in her thirties with a master's degree, who had become alcoholic, depressed, and homeless.

COUNSELOR: So what will your life look like when the problems that brought you here are all behind you?

CLAUDIA: I don't know. I wouldn't be drinking.

COUNSELOR: What else?

CLAUDIA: I wouldn't be so depressed all the time.

COUNSELOR: And what else?

CLAUDIA: I don't know.

COUNSELOR: Let's say that while you are sleeping tonight a miracle occurs, and all the problems that brought you here are solved. When you woke up, what would be the first thing you'd notice that was different?

CLAUDIA: I wouldn't be here!

COUNSELOR: Where would you be?

CLAUDIA: I'd have my own apartment and a job as an instructor at a college. I'd be close to my son, so I could visit him, and I'd be getting along with my ex-husband well enough so it wouldn't be a hassle.

COUNSELOR: What else do you notice?

CLAUDIA: I'm interested in a lot of different things, helping others, music, a prayer group. People don't treat me like a freak. They respect me and admire me.

COUNSELOR: And what else?

CLAUDIA: I'd be more discriminating in the men I get involved with. I'd be waiting longer before having sex. I'd be looking at life more realistically, and I wouldn't get my hopes up so high that I get let down all the time.

COUNSELOR: And what else?

CLAUDIA: I'd have no legal or financial troubles. My debts would be paid off or at least manageable.

COUNSELOR: And what else?

CLAUDIA: I wouldn't have to carry around this hurt all the time, so I wouldn't have to try to drink or have sex to cope with it. And I wouldn't be so hard on myself—I could make mistakes and that would be okay. I would learn from them.

COUNSELOR: What else would you be doing?

CLAUDIA: I'd be looking ahead and around the corner, instead of just doing what seemed like a good idea at the moment.

Though some of the miracle was stated in the negative (not drinking, not being depressed, not having legal and financial problems, and not carrying around a "hurt"), it pretty clearly lays out the outline of a future that both counselor and client can begin to work toward. This exchange has resulted in many possibilities for positively stated long-term goals, and many ideas that will be useful in future sessions.

Positive future goals are a step in the right direction, but they must almost always be clarified so they are specific, observable, within the client's control, and achievable in the immediate future. These types of clarified, short-term goals are the ideal complement to the long-term goals uncovered with the help of miracle questions. The more details you are able to help the client fill in, the more helpful you will be.

When clients offer general goals, follow-up questions can help the client identify specific short-term goals. For example, if a client offers a general goal, such as wanting to be a better husband, a possible follow-up question might be, "When you are a better husband, what will you be doing that you're not doing now?" Responses such as, "I'll offer to go on a weekend outing this month," or "I'll cook dinner next week on the night she comes home from work late," are an indication that you have been helpful to the client in the setting of meaningful, positively stated, and achievable goals.

For another example, if a client says she is going to improve her attitude, you might ask, "What will people notice that is different when your attitude is improved?" Responses such as, "I'll study for two hours every weekend," or "I'll go on at least three job interviews a week" translate into excellent short-term goals.

In a continuation of the previous case study, a future session clarified a highly achievable short-term goal for Claudia.

COUNSELOR: Tell me more about the hurt you described that you carry around.

CLAUDIA: I feel it at some times worse than others; I'm not sure where it comes from.

COUNSELOR: Those times when it's not so bad, what seems to be different? [The counselor is exploring exceptions to the problem.]

CLAUDIA: Usually I'm feeling more self-confidence, like maybe right after I've accomplished something.

COUNSELOR: So setting and meeting goals makes that hurt seem smaller?

CLAUDIA: I guess so.

COUNSELOR: On a scale of one to ten, with ten being the best your self-confidence could be, and one being the lowest it could possibly be, where would you say you are now? [The counselor is using the scaling technique to look toward the future and help clarify goals.]

CLAUDIA: Maybe a three.

COUNSELOR: Three, that's pretty good. What would you have to see happen to make that a three and a half or four?

CLAUDIA: If the project I'm working on now goes over good, I'll be really happy. I've put a lot into it, but I'm really nervous.

COUNSELOR: When is it?

CLAUDIA: On the fifteenth, the day before our next session.

COUNSELOR: And how would you judge whether it went really well?

CLAUDIA: By attendance. I want at least seven people to be there—ten would be even better.

COUNSELOR: And so if at least seven people show up for your presentation, you'll consider it a success?

CLAUDIA: Not just if they show up, but if they really like it.

COUNSELOR: And how would you know if they really liked it?

CLAUDIA: I could tell by their participation. If they just sit there wishing it's over, that would be a flop, but if they get involved, that would make it a success.

COUNSELOR: So if at least seven people come, and at least five participate, your self-confidence could move up to four?

CLAUDIA: Yes.

COUNSELOR: And you think that's a reasonable and realistic goal?

CLAUDIA: Yes.

This highly clarified and specific goal, if reached, may help build Claudia's self-confidence and ease the hurt she described in an earlier session. The counselor took care to assure that Claudia's goal was realistic for her, one he felt confident she could achieve.

Helping clients clarify goals and look toward the future is one of the greatest rewards of being a counselor. It can generate the same kind of fun and excitement as planning an African safari. The best future-oriented questions are not leading or loaded questions, but are content free. This allows clients the opportunity to identify their own goals. My experience has been that client-generated goals are more enthusiastically pursued than counselor or "mutually agreed upon" goals.

Once clients are clear on where they want to go, they can begin to see that there is not one, but many, ways to get there. Once hopeless clients begin to meet with results they themselves have defined as successful, both their rate of change and their motivation to change tend to increase dramatically.

Chapter 7

Sharing Counseling Notes
with Hopeless Clients

Summarizing at the end of each session or even sharing your actual counseling notes with hopeless clients is an excellent way to build trust. It also helps you to be sure you have the same understanding of a session as your client. By choosing what to emphasize in the case note, the counselor is often able to gently lead the client in a beneficial direction.

Your case notes naturally emphasize what you feel are the most important points of the session. These will generally be the client statements most likely to generate hope. Even when clients feel hopeless, the notes of their counselors can reflect an optimism that will hopefully be contagious. Seeing notes that show that the counselor feels there is hope often promotes hope in the client.

Sharing your counseling notes is an excellent way to communicate with your clients. It helps keep you both on the same wavelength. And any messages, sent or received, that you or your client feel are unclear can be cleared up by the sharing process. Sharing your notes helps some hopeless clients get in touch with progress that they might not have noticed otherwise.

By way of example, a brief portion of a counseling session is offered below, followed by both a written case note and a verbal summary at the end of the session.

COUNSELOR: How are you feeling?

JENNIFER: I'm still obsessing about my ex-husband. He's never treated me with any respect, but I keep going back to him. I still have that fantasy that he could really love me.

COUNSELOR: Do you think he is capable of love?

JENNIFER: No. He's never been; he's too selfish to care about another person. He might like having sex with me, but he has no other use for me.

COUNSELOR: So the kind of relationship that you would like to have with your husband is not an option with Charles?

JENNIFER: I guess not. I still feel really depressed, though.

COUNSELOR: Worse than ever before?

JENNIFER: No, I haven't had fits of crying, and I don't feel that deep hurt inside me, like I do sometimes. But I'm still very sad.

> *Case note:* Jennifer expressed some ambivalence about her ex-husband, Charles. Although she sometimes has fantasies about a reconciliation, she realizes that the kind of relationship she wants with a husband is not possible with Charles.
>
> Jennifer also feels less depressed than she has been lately. She still has feelings of sadness, but the symptoms are not as difficult to deal with as they once were. We will explore ways she can continue this progress and gain even more control over her moods in our next session.

Your actual case note from your previous session might be shared with your client at the beginning of each subsequent session. Or you may sum up verbally at the end of each session what you expect to put in your case note. In the previous example, you might say,

> Okay, let's recap what we've been talking about so I can be sure to record it properly in my case notes. You're feeling ambivalent about going back to Charles, but you realize that what you are hoping for in a husband is not available with Charles. You are still sad sometimes, but not as bad as before, when you cried often and for long periods of time, and when you had a hopeless feeling in the pit of your stomach. Is that fair to say? Maybe next time we can continue by looking at how you managed to make that movement toward being more happy or in control of your moods, and build on that progress.

Sharing case notes allows counselors the opportunity to strengthen clients' commitment to change, maintain continuity from session to session, and help keep clients focused on their goals. An added benefit to sharing our actual case notes or summarizing what we intend to record for our clients at the end of each session is that it keeps us focused on the positive achievements as well. And we may make more of an effort to be sure our case notes reflect our care, concern, and respect for our clients that is sometimes obfuscated by DSM jargon.

The idea is *not* to put words into clients' mouths or trick them into looking at things exactly as you would like them to. Rather, the counselor's generally enthusiastic and optimistic perspective is shared for confirmation or rejection by the client. Clients should be encouraged to correct you whenever they feel you have misrepresented what they are thinking.

Chapter 8

Homework

Homework is a mutually agreed upon task to be performed by the client between sessions (Berg and Reuss, 1998). "Real life" offers our clients many more opportunities to grow than all our therapy sessions put together. Homework helps clients take advantage of these learning opportunities, and then process what has been learned in the next session. Treatment works best when it is clearly connected in the client's mind to life outside counseling sessions. Sometimes stuck clients are not connecting their therapy to their real-life problems.

The type of homework most successful with hopeless clients is very specific, identified by the client as being helpful, and almost certain to be accomplished. For hopeless clients, homework can be any task that might help the client believe that change is a real possibility. Agreeing on homework as an experiment keeps hopeless clients from feeling like failures if things don't go as expected.

Some homework assignments are designed to *clarify the problem.* When a hopeless client's complaints are vague, a simple homework assignment that asks the client to notice the antecedents and results of the problem behavior can be helpful.

Your client can feel a sense of accomplishment for completing the assignment. Your next session can zero in on exactly what the client wants to be different and how he or she can make this happen.

Homework assignments that ask hopeless clients to notice things they would *not* want to change can also promote hope. If clients agree to homework that asks them to *notice and record things in their life they are satisfied with,* it helps counter the idea that everything is wrong.

Pattern intervention is a homework assignment in which the client agrees to do something—almost anything—different, to interrupt the problem cycle. The classic story of pattern interruption homework involves a man who complains that he just can't help pulling into the parking lot of his favorite bar, which he passes every day on his way home from work. His homework assignment: Try going home a different way.

If you use the exploring exceptions technique during your session, you might agree to homework that calls for the client to do more of the specific things that have already worked to some degree. For example, if taking a few deep breaths worked at any time to reduce stress, the homework might call for trying deep breaths in all stressful situations.

The scaling technique will often result in appropriate homework, as your clients describe what specific steps they might take between sessions that will bring them higher on the scale. It is used regularly at our Stop Smoking Group.

CASE STUDY: STOP SMOKING GROUP HOMEWORK

Stop Smoking Group members take turns rating themselves on the one to ten scale, explain their reasons for the rating, define goals that will bring them higher on the scale (or in some cases maintain them where they are), and devise tasks they agree to perform as homework. The following is the list of homework assignments from some recent groups.

From a group member who had quit but relapsed: Make a list of the ways I overcame the urge to smoke for the time that I was quit; think carefully about the circumstances I first smoked again and write out a plan for what I might have done instead; decide by next group on a plan to quit again or try to limit the amount I smoke.

From group members who were trying to cut down the number of cigarettes they smoked: Skip the early morning cigarette and the one before bed; instead of going out during those smoking times, brush my teeth; try to smoke no more than ten cigarettes a day; switch to a menthol brand (I hate menthol), and log all the times I smoke; talk with other group members if I feel like smoking more than ten.

From a group member struggling to remain abstinent: Continue relaxation exercises every morning to help relieve stress; make a list of all the things I like better about not smoking and read it every morning; think about how badly I'll feel if I go back to smoking; eat a hard candy or stay upstairs during all smoking breaks.

From a group member who made a firm decision to quit during the next week: Get the patch from the nurse and stop completely on Thursday; on the Wednesday before smoke as many cigarettes as I can, so I'll be disgusted and fed up with smoking; write a letter to my parents telling them I'm quitting, so I'll be less likely to back out.

From a first-time attendee, not sure if she wanted to quit or not: Reread the material on how smoking contributes to wrinkles and varicose veins [lung cancer and heart disease weren't as big a concern!]; make a list of what else I could buy for the amount I spend a month on cigarettes.

SECTION II:
MEETING THE CHALLENGE
OF CLIENTS "IN DENIAL"

Denial has been defined as "a lack of acknowledgment or nonacceptance of important aspects of reality or one's own feelings, impulses, thoughts, or experiences" (Goldstein and Noonan, 1999, p. 41). Built into this definition is the highly questionable idea that counselors are in a better position to be in touch with clients' feelings, impulses, thoughts, or experiences than the clients themselves. And it makes the counselor of every client the ultimate arbiter of "reality."

Some counselors see "breaking through denial" as a big part of their jobs. But just as reframing a client's personal problem may be helpful, reframing our professional problem may be helpful. "Resolving a disagreement about the nature of the client's problem," for example, sounds like a much more pleasant task than "breaking through denial." We are bound to approach it with a more cooperative attitude and with a greater expectation of success. Our willingness to resolve a difference of opinion shows respect for those we serve, and a refusal to blame clients for any lack of progress in treatment.

The idea of clients being in denial has such staying power because the way some of the theories are constructed makes it virtually impossible to prove them wrong. These theories can be very seductive. They make the counselor always "right" and the client always "wrong."

If the client eventually gives in to our perspective on things, it is seen as proof that we were right. If the client disagrees violently and leaves treatment altogether, it is seen as proof that we were right. Any result in between can be described as proof that we were right: We are making some progress with our confrontation of the denial, but there is still a tough road ahead. These theories of denial are claimed to be affirmed whether they're helpful to the client or not.

Denial is the label given to one form of resistance. It does not seem to be a very helpful idea. Like the word "resistant," use of the word "denial" sets up a confrontational rather than cooperative client-counselor relationship. We may be tempted to dismiss or misconstrue much of what the client is saying as additional evidence supporting the perception that he or she is in denial.

Chapter 9

Listening, Alternate Definitions of Denial, and Preferred Views

LISTENING

I believe listening is the single most powerful therapeutic technique at a counselor's disposal. By listening, I mean *really* listening, to understand the client, rather than listening to change the client. As Freedman and Combs (1996) point out in *Narrative Therapy*, counselor listening is often driven by some other goal than hearing what the client has to tell us. These other goals might include case formulation, finding hidden strengths, or identifying defense mechanisms.

Whatever our additional agenda is, it takes away from really hearing what the client has to say. As Freedman and Combs (1996) put it,

> If we think of ourselves as experts on pathology, we will notice, remember, and inquire further about things people say that sound pathological to us. If our listening is guided by a theory that says people must "feel their pain" in order to be whole, we will bring forth painful stories. If we have a special interest in disempowerment as an issue, we will invite people to tell us stories of how they have been deprived of power. (p. 46)

Likewise, if we're listening to identify distorted cognitions, assess ego strength, determine patterns of relating, uncover family dysfunction, identify skill deficits, log relapse triggers, identify defense mechanisms, discover hidden strengths, assess employability, find cognitive deficits, identify coping mechanisms, or heal the wounded inner child, we are less likely to hear what the client is really saying. We should be listening to hear what our clients are saying, not to validate our own theories of change or our favorite therapeutic techniques.

Listening is important, because what our clients have to say is important. Finding out what the client really wants from treatment may be the single most important piece of information that can come out of any counselor-client interaction (Duncan, Hubble, and Miller, 1997). The techniques described in this section are most effective *after* we have listened and heard this information. Once we have acknowledged and validated the client's view and agreed on the goals of treatment, we can begin listening in the way most helpful to furthering our shared agenda.

ALTERNATE DEFINITIONS OF DENIAL

What do therapists mean when they label a client as in denial? It has been my experience that they may mean many different things:

1. *The client and I disagree about the nature of the problem.* Any client's presence in treatment is a request for help with a problem. The counselor and client often have very different definitions of that problem. For example, the counselor may define the problem as alcohol dependence, whereas the client defines the problem in terms of doing what is necessary to stay out of jail, keep a job, or satisfy a nagging spouse.

2. *The client and I notice some of the same things, but interpret or weigh them differently.* Denial is sometimes attributed to clients who think their substance abuse problems have a lower priority than the counselor does. For example, the client may feel dealing with the loss of a loved one has a higher priority than maintaining sobriety.

3. *On some level the client knows there is a serious problem, but refuses to admit it to others.* Many times counselors are of the opinion that their clients know fully well that they are alcoholics and are aware of the problems alcohol is causing in their lives. These counselors may see it as important that the clients admit to this awareness publicly. The client's acceptance of the label of alcoholic or addict is so important to some counselors that they refuse to recognize any other signs of progress.

4. *I know better than the client what is wrong, and the client is too stubborn or proud to agree with me.* Counselors would have no rea-

son to accept clients if the counselors didn't feel that they had something helpful to offer. When counselors become convinced that they have more insight into their clients than the clients themselves, they may describe the client as being in denial.

5. *This client is not respectful enough of my professional opinions.* Counselors may feel that their training and experience in dealing with addicts has provided them with a body of knowledge that is worthy of respect. They may attach the label of denial to those clients whom they feel disregard or devalue what they have to offer.

6. *This client does not enjoy being confronted with his or her past mistakes.* In an effort to assist the client by connecting undesired consequences to substance abuse, heavily confrontational approaches offer clients the opportunity to get in touch with the seriousness of their substance abuse problem. When clients do not appreciate these efforts on their behalf, it is sometimes called denial.

The term "denial" makes it sound like a one-sided phenomenon. In each of the alternative definitions just given, denial is an interactional phenomenon. That is, none of these definitions can be applied outside a counseling relationship. In each definition, it takes two to make denial.

This sets up a power struggle where only one person can come out the winner. The counselor wins by getting the client to admit to the problem as the counselor sees it, or the client wins by avoiding such an admission. Many clients choose to leave treatment rather than lose. For those who choose to remain, it is not until later in treatment that they express their appreciation for the results of the confrontations.

The people for whom confrontation of denial is the best approach probably wouldn't present for treatment, because they would have already responded to the confrontations of their loved ones, employer, or the legal system. Many counselor attempts to get clients to "face up" to their drinking problem are a continuation of an already tried and failed strategy.

When confrontation does get the desired results, it is often damaging to the client's self-efficacy. Clients learn that they couldn't take full responsibility for their own lives, because it was only through the caring confrontation of others that they were saved. Changes that clients make on their own are the most lasting (Miller, Hubble, and Duncan, 1997).

When we win confrontations with our clients, we undermine their confidence and respect for their own opinions. It becomes clients' perception that it was through an outside source (the efforts of the counselor rather than their own) that they have turned their lives around. When we rely upon clients' own power of reason and ability to make good choices, we help lay the foundation for a high-quality recovery.

When we help clients become realistically confident that they can make good choices, we have done them a great service. If we convince clients to subordinate their judgments to those of others, we may have done them irreparable harm.

It's not fair to label a client's reservations about our preferred models and therapeutic techniques as denial or resistance to change. Clients often offer us an alternative to dealing directly with a problem they are not ready to deal with. A few of the alternative problems proposed by clients include keeping their jobs, reducing arguments with their spouses, avoiding hangovers, regaining custody of their children, and avoiding arrest. When we are willing to work with what the client sees as the problem, we increase the likelihood that what we see as the problem will be addressed along the way.

PREFERRED VIEWS

We all have "preferred views" (Eron and Lund, 1996): the way we look at ourselves and the world around us; the way we want others to view us. When a preferred view is challenged, most people react by defending it. Even very young children seem to know that if they say to a parent, "You don't love me!," parents will often get distracted from the task at hand and defend their view of themselves as loving parents.

One of the preferred views most of us in the counseling profession share is the idea that we *really care* about our clients. When a client accuses us of not caring, it often throws us off track. We may stop listening to our clients and, instead, put our energy into explaining that we care. Counselors may distract clients in much the same way.

If we challenge strongly held preferred views of our clients, or confront them on their denial, we are almost certain to generate resistance. Clients will most likely spend a considerable amount of time and energy defending their preferred views, and we will expend a considerable amount of time and energy challenging them. The time we spend challenging our clients' preferred views, and the time they spend defending them, might be spent in more productive and beneficial interactions. It is easier to build the foundation of a therapeutic alliance by exploring common ground rather than differences of opinion.

Once clients realize that you are taking what they say seriously, they may accept more responsibility for what they say. Without the expectation that we will argue with them, clients may be more likely to tell us what they really think.

This is not to say that we should pretend to agree with everything our clients say, only that we show a genuine interest in and respect for what our clients think. Proceed on the assumptions that: (1) clients are offering the truth as they see it; (2) this is one of many possible explanations; and (3) clients may have good reasons to believe it. Paradoxically, this respect for what the client thinks seems to make it easier for clients to change what they think.

CASE STUDY: UNREALISTIC OPTIMISM

Theresa was relatively new to our program and had a history of bad relationships, inability to maintain a job, and chronic relapse.

THERESA: I've worked on my shame issues, and I don't think it's a problem anymore.

COUNSELOR: Good. How did you manage to handle that so quickly?

THERESA: Well, I'm no longer drinking or being promiscuous, and that was the main basis for my shame.

COUNSELOR: So it just kind of disappeared on its own, once you had the chance to get your head together and stay clean for a few weeks?

THERESA: Yes. I don't see myself staying here very long. It's not like I need a total overhaul of my personality or anything.

COUNSELOR: Great! In what way might the program be helpful to you?

THERESA: I'm not sure.

COUNSELOR: If you left now, do you think you would maintain abstinence?

THERESA: Yes.

COUNSELOR: And do you think you would be able have satisfying relationships and keep a satisfying job?

THERESA: Yes.

COUNSELOR: So it sounds like you have more reasons to leave the program than to stay.

THERESA: [After pausing to reflect] I don't know. Are you kicking me out?

COUNSELOR: No, of course not. I'm just trying to identify an area where we might be helpful to you. Some of the main reasons people come to residential treatment are to work toward an ability to maintain abstinence, have satisfying relationships, and be successful at their jobs. Since you are already competent in these areas, I was just trying to find out where it is you think we can be of help.

THERESA: [After some reflection] To see if I'm right about what I think. I've left other programs before I really should have, because I thought everything was okay.

COUNSELOR: I could be helpful by double-checking what you say about everything being okay?

THERESA: Yes.

COUNSELOR: Has it been a problem for you in the past, kind of looking at things through rose-colored glasses?

THERESA: Yes.

COUNSELOR: And how was it a problem?

THERESA: I would think everything was going to be okay, or I'd put all my eggs in one basket without any backup plan, and then I'd be devastated if things didn't go as I'd hoped.

COUNSELOR: So it's been a pattern of behavior for you that you are at times unrealistically optimistic about the future. I mean, your optimism is sometimes based more on wishful thinking than reality?

THERESA: Yes.

COUNSELOR: So we might be helpful to you by going over those areas in more detail in future sessions—the ability to maintain abstinence, have satisfying relationships, keep a good job—to see if you're being overly optimistic?

THERESA: Yes.

Theresa has, in her own way, *requested* her counselor to confront her denial. The counselor has succeeded in getting this invitation by respecting, rather than challenging, her preferred view. Rather than generate resistance by challenging her statement that she could succeed outside residential treatment, the counselor respected Theresa's perspective on things and held her accountable for it.

It's possible that Theresa, a veteran of several other treatment programs, expected to be challenged on her view of things. She seemed really caught off guard by the validation and acceptance the counselor gave to her. But challenging Theresa's statements could have encouraged reliance on the counselor's judgment instead of her own. Once given the opportunity and responsibility to rely on her own judgment, Theresa opened up the door for a very good suggestion as to how her counselor might be helpful. She was not only "included in the treatment planning," but an actual co-author.

Perhaps we could add "unrealistically optimistic about the future" to our alternate definitions of denial. If we listen closely to our clients, they will teach us hundreds of other alternate definitions.

Chapter 10

Consciousness Raising

Some clients said to be in denial simply do not have the information necessary to recognize or realize the severity of their problem. Consciousness-raising techniques may be helpful in providing this information.

Consciousness-raising involves increased awareness and information about the causes, consequences, or solutions for a particular problem (Hubble, Duncan, and Miller, 1999). The following techniques have been successful in raising clients' levels of awareness of the benefits of change. This sometimes works to motivate clients referred to as in denial to begin to address a problem.

DEVELOPING DISCREPANCY

Developing discrepancy is an extension of the idea of cognitive dissonance. As explained in *Motivational Interviewing* (Miller and Rollnick, 1991, p. 57),

> A more general and, we believe, a better way to understand this process is simply as a discrepancy between where one is and where one wants to be. This can be triggered by an awareness of the costs of the present behavior. When a behavior is seen as conflicting with important personal goals (such as one's health, success, family happiness, or positive self image), change is likely to occur.

The idea is to avoid a frontal attack on the preferred view, which would likely generate resistance, and instead help clients realize that what they are doing is interfering with their personal goals.

One way to develop discrepancy is the "mystery question" recommended by Joseph B. Eron and Thomas W. Lund (1996) in *Narrative Solutions in Brief Therapy*. The formula for a mystery question is something like this: How did someone with X (client's preferred view of self) wind up in situation Y (client's preferred view of problem), and being viewed by others as Z (challenges to the client's preferred view)? The idea is to use what you have learned about clients' preferred views and ask for their help in figuring out how they wound up having a problem and being viewed by others in ways they don't like.

An example of a mystery question is, "How does it happen that a good mother like you, who wants to see to it personally that her children have the best of everything, attracts so much attention from social workers who question her ability as a parent?" If you show your client you are genuinely interested in her help in solving this riddle, you can begin a collaboration and avoid a confrontation.

This type of question respects the preferred view of the client, while opening up the possibility of raising awareness of what behaviors may be interfering with personal goals. If your client expresses a willingness to change some of the behaviors most likely to attract the attention of child welfare workers, for example, the client is on her way to resolving the discrepancy.

EXAMPLES OF MYSTERY QUESTIONS

Here are some examples of how preferred views might be incorporated into mystery questions with several different populations.

- *For complaints about the workplace:* "How is it that a hard-working and dedicated employee such as yourself would be so underappreciated by co-workers?"
- *For those with marital difficulties:* "How is it that a person like you, who really wants to work on his marriage, would be getting such a lack of cooperation from his wife?"
- *For adolescents:* "Why is it that an intelligent young man like yourself, who has expressed an interest in going to college, being viewed by his teachers as so uncooperative?"

Mystery questions work best when you are genuinely interested in what the client has to say. Mystery questions are likely to backfire when your tone is sarcastic or if you present the question in a confrontational or adversarial "gotcha" kind of way. Your tone of voice should be sincere and inquisitive. You should sound like a student trying to learn about how to be helpful, and not like a prosecuting attorney trying to convince a jury of your client's guilt.

CASE STUDY: BACKSTABBERS

Melanie was an adolescent who might typically be described as in denial. She seemed to believe that the causes of all her problems were outside herself. The group therapy leader attempted to develop discrepancy in the case study below.

MELANIE: Nobody here is supportive of me. They nitpick and constantly badger me.

SYLVIA: You're not willing to accept any responsibility for what you do. [Sylvia is directly challenging Melanie's preferred view.]

MELANIE: I try *so* hard. But nobody here wants to see me succeed. There's not even anybody I can talk to that will sympathize with me. Sometimes I really need to talk and there's nobody.

MONICA: What about your counselor? She'll listen.

MELANIE: No, she won't. I'm asking for a counselor change, and the clinical director is going to assign me another counselor who will be more willing to help me.

JESSICA: Well, I'd be willing to listen if you're upset. I went through some of the same things as you when I first got here.

MELANIE: Yeah, sure. And anything I tell you I'll hear about later. Everybody will know. You're all a bunch of backstabbers. [Melanie is unwilling to consider any input that conflicts with her strongly held preferred view that others are to blame for her lack of progress in treatment.]

GROUP LEADER: So you feel like you are often singled out by others in the house to be held up to ridicule. When you try to have positive discussions, others either won't listen, or if they do listen, they betray your confidence. [The group leader is reflecting back to Melanie his understanding of what she is saying.]

MELANIE: That's right. There's little cliques that stick together, but nobody's there for me. [Melanie confirms that the group leader has understood her view of the problem.]

GROUP LEADER: And even though people in the house are supportive of others, you have to struggle on your own, because when you're involved, they're only interested in being backstabbers.

MELANIE: [crying] Yes.

GROUP LEADER: Well, let's put our heads together and see if we can figure out what it is about you that brings out the backstabber in people.

The group leader's tone is sincere. He has avoided creating denial by his genuine interest in Melanie's view of her situation. The discussion with the group leader has brought out a discrepancy between two things Melanie is saying are both true: (1) There is no possibility of me getting any positive support from others, and (2) I have seen other people find ways to get positive support.

The discrepancy is developed, not by challenging Melanie's view, but by expressing a sincere interest in it. Melanie's idea that her situation was completely beyond her control was not compatible with her view that other clients had found ways to make connections with helping relationships. The group leader has successfully changed the focus from the behavior of others (over which Melanie has no control) to ways in which Melanie might act differently to solve her problem of lack of support.

DECISIONAL BALANCE SHEETS

To most clients referred to as in denial, the benefits of drinking or using drugs seem to far outweigh the benefits of quitting. But they've never really had an opportunity to process this decision with a neutral party. With their drug buddies or friends at the bar, only the "good times" get discussed. With certain family members and counselors, only the bad things about using are open for discussion.

Decisional balance sheets (Miller and Rollnick, 1991) are sometimes helpful in raising clients' level of awareness about the risks of continued substance abuse. It seems to work best when the counselor resists the temptation to argue that clients should not continue to use substances. With a safe place to talk about reasons for and against continued substance abuse, clients sometimes decide to limit or discontinue substance use on their own.

A willingness to give your client room to discuss the enjoyable aspects of substance use is considered by some to be a high-risk strategy. But decisional balance sheets usually don't work with clients considered to be in denial when the counselor takes the position, "think hard about all the bad things about using so you can see how important it is to quit." This approach often generates resistance and a replay of the same arguments that have been unproductive in the past.

Exploring both sides of the argument communicates to clients that you trust them to make the decision, and reinforces the idea that they (and not you nor anyone else) are responsible and accountable for their decisions.

Decisional balance sheets are divided into four sections: short-term negative consequences, short-term benefits, long-term risks, and long-term benefits. Decisional balance sheets can be helpful in several ways. By identifying the benefits of drinking, the client provides possibilities for treatment goals: ways the client might get the same benefits some other way. For example, if, with the counselor's help, a client identifies alternate ways to relax and belong to a social network, it may make the decision to control or discontinue substance use more likely.

Decisional balance sheets can be helpful in raising awareness of many types of problems. Also, as the following case study shows, rather than being uninformed about long-term risks, many clients are really experts on the long-term effects of their problem behavior.

CASE STUDY: DECISIONAL BALANCE SHEETS

Elizabeth was an adolescent client who came to the attention of staff because of reports of self-induced vomiting after meals. She was clearly surprised by her counselor's first request of their session: "Tell me all the good things about throwing up after meals."

Decisional Balance Sheet

1. Short-Term Risks   **2. Short-Term Benefits**

3. Long-Term Risks   **4. Long-Term Benefits**

Elizabeth had just assumed that it was the counselor's job to discuss the bad things about throwing up after meals. She explained that it made her feel like she was back in control; it kept her weight down; and it was something she was good at. The only short-term drawback, to her mind, was the embarrassment of being overheard vomiting and being reported to staff.

Her list of long-term risks demonstrated an impressive understanding of what would happen if she continued: her teeth would fall out; her throat and stomach would bleed; she could develop an irregular heartbeat or even suffer cardiac arrest.

The decisional balance sheet seemed to help, in part because it put into words Elizabeth's ambivalence about purging after meals. And it confirmed something she really already knew: what seemed like a good idea in the short run was not a good idea in the long run.

Still, the decisional balance sheet did not have the immediate effect of a change in Elizabeth's purging. What it did provide were some mutually agreed upon goals that included finding other ways to feel in control, maintain her desired weight, and enjoy the feeling of being good at something.

Some may have viewed Elizabeth as in denial about her eating disorder, and even with the decisional balance sheet she did not decide to end all purging after meals. But the exercise did help identify areas Elizabeth *was* willing to work on (increased control over her life, consideration of healthier ways to achieve her desired appearance, and finding hobbies or other activities that helped her feel she was good at something). Using decisional balance sheets to raise awareness of the benefits of change and/or the risks of not changing in certain areas can make a difference in clients' willingness to define and work toward resolving a problem.

Chapter 11

Clarifying Goals and Looking Toward the Future with Clients "in Denial"

Unlike the hopeless clients discussed in Section I, clients considered to be in denial may have a very clear and detailed vision of life without drugs, but it is one that is not realistic for them. They may think they will return to their favorite bar and just drink soda, or only smoke a little pot on the weekends. The challenge is not so much to help clients envision a happy future but to help make that vision a realistic one.

Counselors often see choices that clients make as connected to many of the client's complaints. The "denial" tag is put on many of these clients, because they are seen as being opposed to change. But they are really strong proponents of change. They are often full of suggestions on how their spouses, counselors, and employers should be doing things differently. Or they'd like to change the inescapable consequences of their choices.

The changes some clients want most are changes in other people or in the world around them. When such clients voice complaints or view others as the problem, we can often help by translating this complaint or view into a goal that the client genuinely wants to accomplish.

TURNING COMPLAINTS INTO TREATMENT GOALS

When clients complain of social workers who stick their noses in other people's business, spouses that nag, or "just my rotten luck," try to connect with what result or goal they are really after. What is it they would like to be different? Then agree on what things within the cli-

---

Turning Client Complaints into Treatment Goals

Complaint	Goal
• Everybody hassles me.	• Be freer to make my own choices.
• My wife nags me.	• Have a more understanding relationship with my spouse.
• I just have really rotten luck.	• Increase the odds of more satisfactory outcomes.
• My mother and father just want to keep me locked up in my room.	• Gain the trust of my parents.

---

ent's power to do might accomplish this result. This helps focus on the future and what the client wants, rather than the past and what the client doesn't like.

TURNING CLIENT COMPLAINTS INTO TREATMENT GOALS: PRACTICE AND RESPONSES

Take a moment to consider how you might respond to each of the client complaints below. Once you and your client are in agreement with goals such as these, collaborating on tasks is relatively easy.

***Client complaint:* "My boss picks on me."**
Possible goal:

Client complaint: **"I don't want to be here."**
Possible goal:

Client complaint: **"You can't trust anybody."**
Possible goal:

Client complaint: **"You don't like me."**
Possible goal:

Possible responses are suggested on the next page.

* * *

Client complaint: **"My boss picks on me."**
Possible goal: Be seen as more competent at work.

Client complaint: **"I don't want to be here."**
Possible goal: Complete treatment as soon as possible.

Client complaint: **"You can't trust anybody."**
Possible goal: Develop more supportive friendships.

Client complaint: **"You don't like me."**
Possible goal: Command respect from others.

Chapter 12

Other Techniques

EXTERNALIZING WITH CLIENTS "IN DENIAL"

Many of the clients said to be in denial use creative words or phrases that represent their problem, but which also allow them a face-saving way to avoid the explicit statement, "It's all my fault." Often what the client is doing is externalizing the problem in much the same way as discussed in Chapter 5.

Some counselors may view discussion of "a dark cloud that follows me around" as an attempt to avoid responsibility. Some traditional approaches would focus on efforts to get these clients to accept responsibility for their actions by helping clients connect the problematic behaviors with their undesirable results. Having raised the client's awareness of this connection, counselor and client would collaborate on a plan of action.

In the best-case scenario the counselor explains, "It's not a dark cloud, it's *you!*" The client rejoices in the realization that the counselor is right, thanks the counselor for providing such wonderful insight, and fully cooperates in treatment from then on.

Of course, the more likely scenario is the generation of resistance. Most clients already know, on some level, that their choices matter. But they may be uncomfortable discussing with you just how bad their choices have been. Such a client may be signaling you that it is easier to discuss this matter in terms of a black cloud that follows them (or an anchor that holds them down, a dark side, a black hole or void that sucks them in, a Mr. Hyde, etc.). A willingness to work within such metaphors often brings positive results, with far less danger of generating resistance.

Rather than help clients disclaim any responsibility for their problems, externalizing actually helps them accept responsibility. As Bill O'Connell (1998) notes in *Solution-Focused Therapy,*

> The client can, for example, have a greater sense of agency and power whereas previously there was a passive-victim stance.... Externalization can also help decrease conflict and blame about ownership of and responsibility for the problem. Without discounting accountability, it is possible to talk about the problem in a way which does not personalize it and thus invite blame, defensiveness, and self-justification. (p. 81)

CASE STUDY: THE BEAST WITHIN

Rita was a thirty-five-year-old with a history of drug use and violence. She spoke in group about a "monster" that she could not control.

RITA: I don't know. It's like there's a monster inside me that I just can't control. I try to keep it down, but then other people do things that let it out.

GROUP LEADER: Tell me more about how you try to keep the monster down.

RITA: Well, I know it real good. I know when to be on my guard, because certain kinds of things just set the monster off.

GROUP LEADER: What types of things?

RITA: Like when people piss me off. I could take it one, two, maybe three times. But then the monster takes over and makes me lose my temper.

The group leader worked within the metaphor Rita had provided to explore several ideas for dealing with what Rita referred to as the monster. They talked about setting it free, but Rita decided against that idea because it could always come back, and she'd never know when.

The group leader brought up the idea of killing the monster, which seemed to upset Rita. Even though the monster makes her do bad things, she explained, they've been together for so long that she wouldn't want it dead.

GROUP LEADER: So, then, what would be the best way to deal with this monster?

RITA: Maybe I could tame it and sort of keep it as a pet. [The group laughs aloud at this suggestion.]

GROUP LEADER: That sounds like a really good idea. It could be like a watchdog that barks when it thinks you should know something. But it wouldn't be like a wild dog that really hurts people. Do you really think you could tame this monster?

RITA: I'd have to think about it.

Rita has agreed to think about taming her monster. She might not have been so agreeable to a suggestion that she is a very angry person and she needs to find ways to deal with her suppressed rage.

Clients seem to use these externalizations for as long as they find them useful. Some use them only to help them get over an initial reluctance to talk about themselves. Others wait until *after* they have made big changes in themselves.

Rita eventually came to the conclusion that she and her monster had a lot in common. Both liked to ride motorcycles, and neither took any guff (Rita used a different word) from anybody. After years of struggle with the monster, Rita began to look in new ways at what she might do to help keep it under her control.

SHARING COUNSELING NOTES
WITH CLIENTS "IN DENIAL"

Sharing counseling notes with clients considered to be in denial offers many opportunities to be helpful. It is a way to build trust with clients generally considered distrustful. Consider the following brief exchange and the two possible case note records provided.

COUNSELOR: Why have you decided to see me?

HARRY: The judge thinks I'm an alcoholic.

COUNSELOR: And what do you think?

HARRY: I know I'm not. I'm sure the charges against me are a mistake. I did have a few drinks before getting into the car, but I'm a big man and I can handle my liquor quite well. I wasn't driving erratically, but was stopped because my tail light was out. The cop smelled liquor on my breath, and that was that.

COUNSELOR: So, if you're only here by mistake, what do you propose we do with our time together? There doesn't seem to be any way I can be of service to you.

HARRY: Maybe you could help me with my temper; I fly off the handle sometimes.

COUNSELOR: Is this when you are drinking?

HARRY: *No!* It has nothing to do with drinking—drinking mellows me out. Sometimes—totally unrelated to alcohol—I blow my stack and am sorry for it later.

> *Possible case note #1:* The client is in denial about his drinking. He refuses to take responsibility for his actions or acknowledge the obvious consequences. He refuses to accept the fact that his angry outbursts are directly tied to the times he hasn't had a drink, and that unless he handles his drinking problem, he will never be able to handle his temper. Until this client is willing to accept responsibility for his alcoholism and his treatment, further sessions are unlikely to be helpful.

Sharing this case note with the client is unlikely to be helpful. It is discouraging, rather than encouraging, and unlikely to be met with acceptance by the client. The same session might be better summarized this way:

> *Possible case note #2:* The client feels strongly that he has no problem with alcohol, and that his mandate to treatment is a

mistake. Even so, he has decided to take advantage of his mandate to work on something he would like to change. He would like to be less of a "hothead" and be able to handle his temper in ways that he's not sorry for later on. We will work together to identify alternatives for better ways to handle anger.

The first case note reflected the counselor's belief that Harry's anger was the result of his dependence on alcohol, and that he blew his top when he had to go without a drink. The counselor's theory is that if Harry faces up to his alcohol dependence, and maintains abstinence long enough, going without alcohol will no longer make him angry.

The second case note reflected the counselor's willingness to accept the possibility that if Harry was able to gain better control over his anger, he might no longer feel compelled to drink to "mellow out." Both theories are plausible, but the client is much more open to one than the other.

The court wants to protect society from any further drinking and driving on the part of this client. The counselor wants to help the client make positive changes. And the client wants to deal better with his anger and avoid jail. Sharing the second case note with the client is much more likely to contribute to a preferred outcome for the mandating party, the counselor, and the client.

SECTION III:
MEETING THE CHALLENGE
OF MANDATED CLIENTS

It's not helpful to make assumptions about the level of motivation or likelihood of cooperation based on the fact that a client has been mandated to treatment. One resistance-generating assumption is that mandated clients don't want real change. It is easy to dismiss the assertion by mandated clients, arrested for the fourth or fifth time, that they have now really "learned their lesson" or "seen the light." But there is no reason to assume that our mandated clients are not doing their best under difficult circumstances, and that part of these difficult circumstances is their attendance in a treatment program they only chose as a lesser of two evils.

As the authors of *Changing Addictive Behaviors* attest,

> It is commonly assumed that substance abusers in general, and especially those who are coerced into treatment, particularly by the courts for some substance-related offense, are not motivated for treatment, are less likely to comply with treatment recommendations, are more likely to drop out of treatment, and have poorer overall outcomes. Such individuals are often viewed by treatment staff as merely "putting in their time," with little likelihood of clinical benefit. This conventional wisdom is predicated on the belief that substance abusers cannot be helped until they "want to change" and that they have to be intrinsically motivated at the point of treatment entry if they are to engage in, comply with, and benefit from treatment. . . .

> Fortunately, this does not appear to be the case . . . it may be difficult to distinguish those who enter treatment voluntarily from those who are coerced or mandated with respect to the treatment process or outcome measures. A number of studies have found relatively few differences between individuals who were and were not mandated into treatment with respect to program compliance and treatment outcomes. . . .
>
> When differences were found, they often *favor* the mandated clients. (italics added, Tucker, Donovan, and Marlatt, 1999, pp. 140-141)

In several important ways, the best approach with mandated clients is no different from the best approach with other clients: identification of common ground and exploration of ways to cooperate to help clients achieve what they want from treatment. Mandated clients always have at least one goal we can share—even if it's only wanting an end to the mandate. Staying out of jail, getting back a license, keeping a job, or regaining custody of children are all admirable goals we can share with our mandated clients.

Reflective listening techniques can be especially helpful with mandated clients. Some mandated clients have never spoken to anyone they respect who took their complaints seriously. They are often desperate to feel heard, and simple reflections let them know that they don't need to spend all their counseling time trying to convince you that some of their complaints are valid. A simple acknowledgement following the reflection, such as "that must have been very difficult for you," is often helpful.

In *Solutions Step by Step*, Insoo Berg and Norman Reuss (1998) offer a unique way to view the relationship among counselor, client, and referral source: approach it in much the same way you would marital therapy. Avoid the temptation to take sides, and try to address the concerns of both with respect.

> Working with a mandated client is similar to working with a husband and wife: It is important not to take sides. The first job is to define the goal of therapy, which is best done through questions that ask for a negotiation of the goal by focusing on the idea of a workable solution. (Berg and Reuss, 1998, p. 134)

Skills you have developed dealing with spouses or families can serve you well in reconciling mandated clients and mandating agencies.

Chapter 13

Clarifying Your Role

DIFFERENTIATING YOURSELF FROM THE REFERRAL SOURCE

Make sure clients are fully aware of the confidentiality laws which allow them to decide whether or not you are able to communicate with the referring party. Stress the voluntary aspect of the client's choice for treatment over the alternatives available, and let your clients know you agree their choice was a good one.

It also can be helpful to distinguish yourself in some way from the referring agency. We often have a lot more in common with the mandated client than the referring party. For example, the judicial system values compliance; we (the mandated client and counselor) value change. We don't just want to please the criminal justice system; we want something better for the client. In this view, we are more closely identified with what the client wants than what the court wants.

When mandated clients view you as an agent of institutional authority, you rarely get an invitation to treat. When clients begin to view you as caring and understanding, a true collaboration is much more likely.

Let your mandated clients know you appreciate how difficult it must be for someone in their circumstances—for whom coming to treatment was the lesser of two evils. The desire to be free from the mandate and make more of their own decisions can be the foundation for collaboration between you and your mandated clients. The following section, Questions for Mandated Clients, offers some ideas on the types of questions that have sometimes worked with mandated clients.

QUESTIONS FOR MANDATED CLIENTS

- What's better already? How have you changed that we can report to the court?
- Can we suggest to the court that changes will continue in this direction?
- How far would we be willing to go? What would we offer them as far as a change in your behavior or outlook?
- What makes parole/probation think I/this program could help you? What do they expect will happen?
- What makes them think you need counseling? What would satisfy them?
- What do they want you to do differently? What will convince them you don't need to come here anymore?
- Who believes you need to change? What do they believe you need to change?
- What would be the smallest amount of change that would be acceptable to satisfy the requirements of your mandate?
- What are the referral source's goals? How will they measure progress?
- What do you think about what they think?
- What will the court/spouse/boss/family do differently when they believe you've changed? How can we prove you've changed?
- How long do you think you'd have to maintain these changes to satisfy the court?
- How would you like to present yourself to the court?
- What strategies might be helpful in dealing with the people complaining about you?
- What can we do to show them that you are at least trying?
- What are your best qualities? What assets do you have that would help us solve this problem?

QUESTIONS FOR THE MANDATED CLIENT'S REFERRING AGENCY

It may also be helpful to ask similar questions to the referring party. Questions such as these may be used:

- What would you like to be different about this client?
- How might this client prove the required changes have been made?
- What specific things would convince you the mandate for treatment was no longer necessary?
- How long would this client have to maintain these changes to satisfy the mandate?
- What type and frequency of reports would you like for this client?
- Have you noticed any improvements in the client since he or she has been mandated to treatment?

Chapter 14

Preferred Views and Compliments

PREFERRED VIEWS OF MANDATED CLIENTS

Challenging preferred views of mandated clients is especially problematic. Generating the type of resistance that inhibits cooperation is bad enough. With mandated clients, challenging preferred views may also generate the type of resistance that renders therapists practically helpless: the situation where the mandated client agrees with every observation or suggestion that we make. When this happens, there is no way to know for sure what the client is really thinking, and our chances of effecting real change are slim.

How does this client view himself or herself? How does this client view the world? How does he or she wish to be viewed by others? Do your best to connect with and respect the client's preferred view. This is part of meeting mandated clients where they are, and not where you wish they were, or where you think they should be.

John L. Walter and Jane E. Peller (2000) write,

> The advantage for the conversation, and for the client, is that generally when clients hear some acknowledgement of their view of themselves, they relax from fear of judgement. With this relaxation, the conversation opens even more and clients feel free to expand within the conversation. (p. 60)

We often demand a client "get real," or "be honest," or "level"—even though we attack almost every opinion the client expresses! Challenging mandated clients' preferred views is almost guaranteed to create resistance—clients will either argue or hide what they really think. The surest way to encourage mandated clients to tell the truth is to listen in a nonjudgmental way, take what they say seriously, and demonstrate a sincere interest in what they really think.

There's a world of difference between a mandated client who is really changing and one who is merely complying. A mandated client is not really a client until he or she invites you to help him or her change. Connecting with the mandated client's preferred view often gets you that invitation.

As the authors of *Escape from Babel* put it,

> Metaphorically speaking, when clients are in the precontemplative stage of change, the therapist has usually not been invited into their house. While the therapist may have many useful suggestions for arranging clients' furniture or decorating their home, such considerations are secondary to gaining admittance. The challenge is that clients in the precontemplative stage frequently have thick doors with strong locks. To be sure, these doors can be broken down or the locks forced. Once in, however, the therapist will likely have to contend with clients in no mood for interior decorating or even entertaining ideas on how it might be done. Mostly, they will be thinking about how to throw the intruder/therapist out. Should clients be compelled to move things around against their will, they will, once the pressure is removed, put the house back the way they prefer.
>
> No doubt, it is better to be invited. (Miller, Hubble, and Duncan, 1997, p. 92)

Simply asking mandated clients for their ideas on how to proceed may affect them very powerfully. They may feel as if nobody they have been involved with values their opinion on how to proceed. When they see that you do, they may invite your involvement. Requesting mandated clients' opinions or even co-writing reports for referring agencies with mandated clients is a step toward helping them build a sense of self-efficacy and trust.

This is not to say that you should pretend to agree with everything your mandated client says, only that you show a genuine interest in and respect for what the client thinks. If you ask the right questions, you can almost always find some common ground you and your client can stand on together.

Again, joining a client and honoring preferred views is *not* the same as agreeing with everything the client says. What seems to be important is that clients understand you are genuinely interested in their point of view. Mandated clients should feel comfortable in the knowledge that you will not ridicule, scold, or judge them for what they think.

COMPLIMENTING THE MANDATED CLIENT

Besides honoring the mandated client's preferred views, sincere compliments may also make it more likely the counselor will get an invitation to help. I think it's reasonably safe to say that if there is one group of clients who are the *least* likely to get sincere compliments, that group is mandated clients. Possibly for this very reason, sincere compliments can be highly effective in encouraging mandated clients to request your help.

For example, you might say to an employee assistance program (EAP) referral, "Even though I can tell you are not completely thrilled about the idea of coming to see me, I am impressed at the willingness you are showing to do what is necessary to keep your job." The many things mandated clients are doing that are good should be highlighted. Clients seem more likely to change in an environment that encourages their strengths than in an environment that focuses on their problems.

Mandated clients may be so used to people criticizing them that a sincere compliment will catch them off guard and become the basis for a truly collaborative relationship (Berg and Miller, 1992). My experience with mandated clients—really with all clients—has been that it's the sense of having accomplished something positive that motivates and provides the self-confidence that makes additional positive changes more likely. Building on this feeling of accomplishment works much more often than "constructive criticism" that puts the emphasis on the room for further improvement.

Chapter 15 offers suggestions for identifying and amplifying change in mandated clients.

Chapter 15

Identifying and Amplifying Change

IDENTIFYING AND AMPLIFYING PRETREATMENT CHANGE

Don't make the mistake of dismissing mandated client reports of pretreatment change. As the authors of *Escape from Babel* observe,

> . . . it seems that once people decide to enter treatment they suddenly become less than they were before. They cease knowing their own mind, are disconnected from their feelings, certainly have "something" wrong with them that requires fixing, and, of course, will do their devilish best to resist the therapists' efforts to help them.
> . . . Nevertheless, the research literature makes it clear that *the client is actually the single, most potent contributor to outcome in psychotherapy. . . .* Clients, the research makes abundantly clear, are the true masters of change in psychotherapy. (italics in original, Miller, Hubble, and Duncan, 1997, p. 24)

Counselors are especially skeptical of mandated clients who report pretreatment changes. But the experience of being arrested and convicted—even if it's for the tenth time—is an environmental factor that often facilitates change. Studies show between 16 and 66 percent of all clients show positive change prior to treatment (Miller, Hubble, and Duncan, 1997). Many people on waiting lists improve so much that treatment is no longer necessary for them. Ask mandated clients what has improved since the event that triggered the mandate. Then work with the client to amplify those pretreatment changes.

Questions and Requests That Help Identify Pretreatment Change of Mandated Clients

When the first session is scheduled:

- It sounds like you've made a good decision as far as calling here; be thinking about other good decisions you've been making lately, and we'll discuss them at our first session.
- Between now and the time of your appointment, please keep track of all the positive things in your life that you'd like to keep going in that direction.

In the first session:

- How are you looking at things differently since your arrest?
- What's gotten better since you made your appointment to come here?
- What have you done since scheduling this appointment that has made your situation better?
- Have you been cited for any additional violations of your parole since you made this appointment? If not, how have you managed to do that?
- How much have you used illegal drugs since making this appointment? Is that more or less than usual? How did you manage to do that? Tell me about the successful strategies you have been using.
- With all that pressure on you, of having to begin a treatment program you'd really rather not be a part of, how did you manage to avoid drinking?
- What do you have to do to keep up this good work?

You want to learn as much as you possibly can about pretreatment change. Clients who report pretreatment change may see themselves as more capable and may be more confident in their ability to change (Miller, Hubble, and Duncan, 1996). The decision to seek treatment, even as an alternative to prison, losing one's license, or termination of parental rights, is a good decision that can be the first in a series of good decisions that leads to quality sobriety. The circumstances that resulted in this decision (including the client's state of mind) often present a "window of opportunity" for clients to make improvements in their lives.

Helping mandated clients uncover pretreatment changes they may have overlooked may help them become more optimistic about and more involved in treatment. Talking about client improvements is an agreeable subject that encourages clients to continue going in a positive direction (Furman and Ahola, 1992). The improvements can be supported and expanded upon using many of the same exploring exceptions techniques discussed in Chapter 4.

IDENTIFYING AND AMPLIFYING
BETWEEN-SESSIONS CHANGE

Just as it may be tempting to dismiss mandated client reports of pretreatment change, between-sessions change is often dismissed as too good to be true—almost surely a sign that the client is anxious to get out of treatment rather than a sign of progress. Again, research indicates that between-sessions change is the rule, rather than the exception (Miller, Hubble, and Duncan, 1997), and this is true for mandated clients as well. Validating and congratulating mandated clients on changes is more effective than focusing on mandated client mistakes. Being arrested often sets in motion a chain of events that leads to improvement (Muller, Hubble, and Duncan, 1997). Counselors should work to recognize and encourage that improvement.

When we focus on what's the same from week to week, it's easy to overlook progress (Miller, Hubble, and Duncan, 1997). Look more closely for what's better in the mandated client's life since the last session. Ask questions such as, "What's different lately?" or "What have you been finding helpful?" and "How did you make that happen?"

Don't let a negative expectation about how difficult mandated clients are keep you from recognizing and encouraging between-sessions changes. Help your mandated clients recognize their unique talents and abilities and how they have successfully put them to use to improve their situations. To highlight between-sessions change, use questions similar to those suggested for exploring pretreatment change.

- How are you looking at things differently since our last session?
- What is better in your life since our last session?
- What have you done since our last appointment that made your situation better?
- How have you managed to maintain abstinence/reduce use between sessions? Tell me, step by step, how you did it. What coping strategies did you employ?

Once again, discussing improvements in the client's situation will rarely generate resistance and will encourage additional changes in a helpful direction.

Chapter 16

Turning Complaints into Treatment Goals and Promises into Treatment Tasks

TURNING COMPLAINTS INTO TREATMENT GOALS

As discussed in Chapter 11, when clients voice complaints or view others as the problem, we can often translate this complaint or view into a goal that the client genuinely wants to achieve. When mandated clients complain of a judge who's an idiot, social workers who stick their noses in other people's business, or parole officers that are just never satisfied, try to connect with what result or goal the mandated client is really after. We can work to turn negative, backward-looking complaints into positive, forward-looking goals.

For example, if the mandated client says, "My parole officer picks on every little thing I do," you might say, "So you'd like to have your parole officer acknowledge some of the progress that you've made." If your client agrees with this goal, discuss what things within the mandated client's power might accomplish this result.

Following are some additional examples of turning mandated client complaints into treatment goals. Once your client is in agreement with any one of the goals, collaborating on tasks is relatively easy.

Take a moment to consider how you might turn the following client complaints into treatment goals. One possible response to each client statement is provided at the end of this chapter.

Turning Mandated Client Complaints into Treatment Goals

Complaint	Goal
• My parole officer picks on every little thing I do.	• Acknowledgment of my progress by parole officer.
• The Department of Social Services is really out to get me; they won't get off my back.	• Regain custody of my children.
• The stupid judge suspended my license.	• Get my license back.
• I shouldn't even be here; my boyfriend is the one who sold the drugs.	• Make better choices of significant others; have more successful intimate relationships.

TURNING MANDATED CLIENT COMPLAINTS INTO TREATMENT GOALS: PRACTICE AND RESPONSES

Client complaint: **"My boss picks on me."**
Possible goal:

Client complaint: **"I just have bad luck."**
Possible goal:

Client complaint: **"I don't want to be here."**
Possible goal:

Client complaint: **"You don't like me."**
Possible goal:

Another way to help mandated clients turn complaints into treatment goals is to ask how they would react if the people they are complaining about did change, and acted how clients thought they should act. Often, they will explain that if the others acted differently, then they would be able to act the way they really want to, and these could become treatment goals.

For example, you might ask, "If your boss did get off your back, how would that affect you? What would you be doing differently?" When the response reveals a strong desire to perform well on the job, proceed by asking how this might be accomplished in spite of the boss remaining the same.

Likewise, a question such as, "When the legal system is off your back, and you are no longer being so closely monitored, how will you be acting differently?" may often be helpful. In my experience, the response has almost never been a desire to return to illegal activities. The follow-up questions zero in on how to have the kind of life the client really wants, in spite of the intrusive nature of the legal mandate.

TURNING PROMISES INTO TREATMENT TASKS

With mandated clients, it is often helpful to use reflective listening techniques to be sure that you are both translating the client's general statements into the same specifics. For example, client and counselor may have totally different ideas about what "staying out of trouble" means. You might want to include in your reflection some specific ways to measure the staying out of trouble, for example, "Are you saying you expect to come on time to all your counseling sessions, and have clean urines from now on?"

When mandated clients suggest they won't be hanging out with the same old crowd or will begin looking for work, it is helpful to identify the specifics that these intentions might translate into for your client.

* * *

Client complaint: **"My boss picks on me."**
Possible goal: Be seen as more competent at work

Client complaint: **"I just have bad luck."**
Possible goal: Decrease the odds of getting arrested

Client complaint: **"I don't want to be here."**
Possible goal: Complete treatment as soon as possible

Client complaint: **"You don't like me."**
Possible goal: Command respect from others

Chapter 17

Other Techniques for Mandated Clients

SCALING WITH MANDATED CLIENTS

Scaling is also useful in dealing with mandated clients. Clients can be asked to rate on a scale of one to ten how close they feel they are to satisfying the terms of their mandate. Then they might be asked what would bring them a point or half a point higher on the scale. The goals produced from this discussion should be measurable by both the client and the referral source. As with any short-term goals, they should be meaningful to the client, within the client's control, stated positively, and small.

It is sometimes helpful to use the scaling technique to assess mandated clients' willingness to make specific changes or their confidence that they will change. For example, if a mandated client reported a high willingness to change, but a low confidence, you might agree on tasks to raise the confidence.

Scaling is also helpful to mandated clients when the referral source is unclear about what they are hoping will be accomplished. "Respect for authority" or "a change in attitude" may mean different things to the client, the counselor, and the referring source. Scaling can help the client identify clearly defined measures of progress acceptable to all parties. If the mandated client is also hopeless, the scaling techniques in Section I may also be helpful.

REFRAMING WITH MANDATED CLIENTS

It is sometimes helpful to normalize the hostility and anger some mandated clients bring with them to treatment. Most people who have lost control over some of their choices in life are upset about this. But therapy can often be a way to regain control of one's life. Discussion might center on neutralizing the effects of the anger that are bringing undesired consequences to the client.

Reframing can also help mandated clients view terms of parole, orders of protection, and even the mandate to treatment itself as helpful. For example, an order of protection against a husband may be seen as helping to keep him from being provoked into behaviors that would have consequences the mandated client strongly wants to avoid. If the mandated client is also hopeless, the reframing techniques in Section I may also be helpful.

EXPLORING EXCEPTIONS
WITH MANDATED CLIENTS

One possibly helpful way of exploring exceptions with mandated clients is to zero in on the times between arrests, when they were staying out of trouble. They might attribute these times to luck (and they may be right!), but there are often differences in how they are thinking and acting between the times they get in trouble.

As Berg and Reuss (1998) put it in *Solutions Step by Step,*

> Every DWI offender has had at least one occasion when he had too much to drink, had the keys to his car, and decided not to drive. On this exceptional occasion, the offender was a non-driving drinker. Our job in therapy is to explore this exception and help our client figure out a way to make this exception the rule. (p. 125)

Notice how the goal as described by Berg and Reuss is identical to the goal of the legal system. The goal of avoiding arrest is also likely to be embraced the mandated client.

CASE STUDY: "I COULD IF I WANTED TO"

In a staff-led group during a discussion of her low self-esteem, Jane, a client mandated to treatment by the legal system after violating the terms of her parole, mentioned a period of four months she managed to have clean urines.

GROUP LEADER: How did you manage to accomplish that? Four months of clean urines?

JANE: It was when I still had a chance to get my son back. When they terminated parental rights, I didn't care anymore.

GROUP LEADER: What did you do differently that you were able to avoid using those four months?

JANE: I just stayed away from that crowd, you know, people and places.

GROUP LEADER: So you're saying that it's easier to stay clean if you don't go to certain areas in your city, and if you avoid certain people.

JANE: Yeah, everybody knows that.

GROUP LEADER: And how did you manage to avoid these people and places during those four months?

JANE: It wasn't really that hard. I had a purpose [to get back her son]. I was motivated. I thought I had a chance in life.

GROUP LEADER: So it's easier for you to maintain sobriety when you feel you have a chance for happiness or a goal to work toward.

JANE: Yes. Sometimes you just wonder, "What's the use?" You know what I mean? And that's when you don't care anymore and it doesn't matter if you pick up.

GROUP LEADER: So having something to look forward to and a realistic basis for hope are important for you to stay off drugs?

JANE: I think so.

GROUP LEADER: And what else did you do that four months you were clean?

JANE: I guess I was more honest with myself. I knew I was drinking and drugging too much, and that my son's father was probably just worried about him. I didn't blame everybody else as much for losing custody. I was really trying then.

GROUP LEADER: So it sounds like being honest with yourself, taking responsibility for your actions, avoiding blame, and really trying your best all contributed to this period of sobriety.

JANE: That's right. I know I can do it if I want to. I'm just not sure that I want to.

GROUP LEADER: Well, if you ever *did* decide you wanted to, what would be the first thing you would do?

JANE: If I decided I wanted to, I could get a job and my own apartment.

GROUP LEADER: Did you have a job during this four months of clean urines?

JANE: Some of the time. I worked as a sales clerk at a department store. I can be very friendly and helpful when I want to be.

GROUP LEADER: So staying employed has also proven helpful to you in maintaining sobriety. What else would you do if you ever decided you really wanted to change?

JANE: Well, I guess I'd be more serious about this program. Maybe I should have put that as the first thing I would do. Because I couldn't decide to leave here on my own without going back to jail.

GROUP LEADER: Okay, we've talked about a lot of things, but the most exciting thing to me is that you know you could change if you really wanted to. And you even know a lot of the things you could do to encourage that change. You've talked about avoiding certain people and places, having things to look forward to, being honest with yourself, resisting the temptation to blame others for your troubles, getting and keeping a job, and really getting serious and working the program.

Even though you're not sure if you want to, I think it's exciting that you are in touch with so many of the things you could do if you ever did decide to change.

The group leader explored exceptions with this mandated client, and identified several choices the client had made in her past that impacted her ability to maintain sobriety. Despite what she says, it is possible that part of Jane's reluctance to give her all in the program may be that she *doesn't* really think she can do it. By encouraging discussion of successful strategies, the group leader is hoping to build Jane's sense of self-efficacy and increase the likelihood of resolving her ambivalence in favor of making a positive change.

DEVELOPING DISCREPANCY
WITH MANDATED CLIENTS

One way to honor and respect clients' preferred views is to hold them fully responsible for those views. As anyone who works with mandated clients will tell you, you can't totally dismiss the possibility that mandated clients will lie in an effort to get through treatment sooner than they think they could otherwise.

If we gently but persistently question these clients, with genuine curiosity about how what they are saying could be true, they may soon come to the conclusion that they can get their therapy over with sooner by telling the truth. This has been called the Columbo approach (Selekman, 1997), after the television character played by Peter Falk. His polite and nonthreatening manner invites cooperation, and his sincere and persistent questioning generally leads to a happy ending. He just makes it clear that telling the truth ends up being a lot easier than sticking to a story that is not supported by the facts.

EXAMPLES OF MYSTERY QUESTIONS
FOR MANDATED CLIENTS

As Eron and Lund (1996) point out, "Often there's a wide gap between how mandated clients prefer to be seen (independent, autonomous) and how they describe their current predicament (watched closely . . . having no freedom). Inviting clients to explain how they arrived in this troublesome fix is a resistance-proof way to obtain information about the evolution of the problem" (p. 254).

The following are some examples of mystery questions for mandated clients:

- *For clients ordered to treatment as a condition for regaining custody of their children:* "How is it that a caring parent such as yourself should attract so much attention from the child protection agency?"
- *For clients ordered to treatment by an EAP:* "Why doesn't your boss notice and appreciate your job performance, instead of sending you to the Employee Assistance Program?"
- *For a probationer or parolee:* "With all you've done to show you've changed, what more will we have to do to convince the courts you are no longer a 'threat to society'?"

CASE STUDY:
"I CAN'T BELIEVE IT'S NOT BUTTER"

Jill decided to seek treatment as an alternative to prison. She had missed two appointments for admission and was told the third would not be rescheduled.

COUNSELOR: Tell me about the circumstances that contributed to your decision to seek treatment. [The therapist's opening request acknowledges the client's choice in choosing treatment over prison and tries to identify what problems Jill sees with her current lifestyle.]

JILL: I think you know very well why I'm here; the court has mandated me.

COUNSELOR: And that is your only reason for being here?

JILL: Yes.

COUNSELOR: Well, that is a very good reason, and I appreciate your honesty. Sometimes the people sent by a court try to "phony it up" for me, and I appreciate your straightforward manner.

JILL: That's partly why I'm in this mess; I'm too honest.

COUNSELOR: What do you mean?

JILL: I don't take any crap from anybody—not cops, not judges, not my husband. I know who I am, and I won't change just to suit anybody else.

COUNSELOR: [The counselor has uncovered a strongly held preferred view.] So this must be very difficult for you, a person with such a strong personality, being forced into treatment.

JILL: No, it's not difficult. I do what I have to do.

COUNSELOR: [The counselor suspects that this *is* difficult for Jill, but decides not to challenge her preferred view at this point.] You sound like a very independent and strong-willed person.

JILL: Yes. And I can tell when someone is trying to butter me up, so don't waste your time. [Jill has challenged the counselor's preferred view of himself and his preferred approach to her.]

COUNSELOR: [Resisting the temptation to defend himself] Well, you're very perceptive. I do try to start out on a good note with all my clients, but with you it seems like I can get right to the point. Tell me about what you'd like to be different in your life.

JILL: I'd like the court and my husband to get off my back.

COUNSELOR: [Turning Jill's complaints into treatment goals] So you'd like to complete treatment as quickly as possible, and have a better relationship with your husband?

JILL: Yes to both.

COUNSELOR: And which of these should we tackle first?

JILL: Getting out of here as quickly as possible.

Jill has invited the counselor to help her, but not all counselors would even notice her willingness to cooperate. They might view a client whose main motivation is to stay out of prison and end treatment as soon as possible as "uncooperative," "not interested in treatment," or "not ready to change." They might think that a "lack of motivation" makes this case nearly impossible.

But clients who want to stay out of jail and who identify stressors such as problems in their marriage *are* motivated. There are many clients who don't care if they go to jail, or don't care if they save their marriage. I know of some clients who don't care how long residential treatment takes; they seem to prefer this relatively sheltered environment to real life. Clients who care about what happens to them are in many ways easier to deal with than clients who don't care.

In this brief conversation, Jill has really given the counselor a lot to go on: She has identified her preferred view of herself as bright, independent, and not to be pushed around. She has identified her marital relationship as a major stressor in her life and expressed willingness to work on this. And she has expressed a desire to complete treatment as quickly as possible.

Jill has even offered the counselor some tips on improving his counseling style. By sharing her comment about being "buttered up," Jill let the counselor know that his approach needs some fine tuning. If the counselor was just buttering Jill up, she's let him know that such tactics can backfire. If the compliment was sincere, the counselor might consult with Jill on ways he could have made his sincerity come through more clearly.

SHARING COUNSELING NOTES
WITH MANDATED CLIENTS

Sharing your counseling notes is an excellent way to build trust with your mandated clients. They won't be distracted by wondering what you're telling the referring agency, or whether or not you are being honest with them in session.

FRED: Since I was arrested for my DWI, it really made me see the light. I know I'll never drink and drive again.

COUNSELOR: That's wonderful! Tell me more about how you were able to accomplish this transformation.

FRED: Well, I was just thinking how embarrassing it was, to me, my family, and my place of business. I don't ever want that to happen again.

COUNSELOR: So even though you don't think you'll drink and drive again, you're open to counseling as a kind of insurance that you won't drink and drive again.

FRED: Right. I want to satisfy the court's requirement and get a clean bill of health from you, so I can go on with my life.

COUNSELOR: Very good! I'm encouraged that you're willing to do whatever it takes to avoid drinking and driving again.

FRED: I am.

> *Case note:* Fred appears to be highly motivated for treatment. He will welcome the suggestions he receives from our treatment program, because he is determined that this will be the last time he is ever in trouble for drinking and driving. At our next session we will discuss the specific suggestions for what Fred is willing to do, above and beyond the requirements of his mandate, to reach his goal.

This case note is respectful of Fred and the opinions he shared in session. The counselor chooses not to challenge Fred's statements about being highly motivated and open to suggestions but, rather, to give Fred the benefit of the doubt and hold him accountable for those statements.

Fred will realize that any backing away from his original promises may reflect poorly upon him in reports to the referring party. At the next session, Fred either will be truly open to suggestions or will have to admit that he was less than honest in the previous session. Either possibility is a step in the right direction.

HOMEWORK FOR MANDATED CLIENTS

Agreement on homework tasks may help prevent misunderstandings that sometimes occur when counselors and clients translate the same general statements into different specifics. As we've already noted, "staying out of trouble" will most likely be agreeable to your clients. But does this mean the same thing to each of them as it does to you?

A homework assignment that confirms what a mandated client is saying about ability to abstain or other desired behavior can be offered as an opportunity to show that the mandating party is wrong that the client needs such close supervision.

Homework can also be assigned to the referring party. Would they be willing to notice and log improvements in body language, respectfulness, anger management, timeliness in reporting, or urine testing?

SECTION IV:
BREAKING YOUR OWN RULES

The authors of *Working with the Problem Drinker* observe, "Very few in the alcohol treatment community have considered that the behaviors, which labels such as 'resistant' and 'in denial' are intended to describe, are at least as descriptive of the traditional alcohol treatment procedures as they are of the problem drinking population" (Berg and Miller, 1992, p. 21).

OUCH! (Sometimes the truth hurts.)

When we begin to view our clients as resistant to our efforts to help, we may have settled into a pattern that is perpetuating the status quo rather than promoting change.This may sound obvious, but when we want our clients to do something different, we might try doing something different ourselves.

Techniques that you are not currently using may be more likely to break a logjam, because they interrupt the pattern of your usual relationship with the client. Overuse of any technique will likely decrease its effectiveness, as it becomes an expected part of your therapeutic routine.

Many studies show that widely varied models and techniques have similar positive results (Hubble, Duncan, and Miller, 1999). So, when your preferred methods are not working as you would hope, a willingness to "break your own rules" of client engagement can sometimes help.

Our field is divided into many different camps; twelve-steppers, behaviorists, cognitive therapists, psychodynamic psychotherapists, narrative therapists, etc. Many of us are protective of our chosen school and critical of the others. Many times this is based on our first-hand experience. But a willingness to utilize the tools of a wide range of approaches provides us with a wide range of opportunities to be helpful to our clients.

When what we have been trying isn't working, what we haven't tried might work better. For example, if you almost never give advice, offer some. If you are often directive and offer specific suggestions, withhold your advice. If you are a narrative therapist who usually works to rewrite your client's life story, try a few behavioral goals that are very specific. Likewise, if you are a behaviorist, try an intervention that is geared to the less concrete goals of personal growth or emotional release. Switching your approach from passive to active, intrapsychic to intrapersonal, or individual to interactional may resolve a treatment impasse (Miller, Hubble, and Duncan, 1997).

The following suggestions are designed to make your therapeutic messages more memorable and to interrupt a less-than-successful pattern of relating to your clients. These might be reserved for use by experienced counselors, when the techniques that have usually been helpful aren't. They are best used sparingly, as overuse of any technique may dilute its effectiveness.

Chapter 18

Utilization

Without mentioning it by name, previous chapters have touched upon the idea of utilization (Berg and Miller, 1992; Duncan, Hubble, and Miller, 1997; O'Hanlon and Beadle, 1997; O'Hanlon and Weiner-Davis, 1989; Selekman, 1997). Utilization involves use of each individual client's unique set of resources and ideas, and being flexible enough to connect in a different way with each client. The idea is to take full advantage of clients' strengths, their innate capacity to grow, and helpful events in clients' lives outside therapy, as well as things most counselors would consider "negatives." This is closely related to the ideas of accommodating the client (Duncan, Hubble, and Miller, 1997) and transferring competence (O'Hanlon and Beadle, 1997) from one area of the client's life to another.

So a counselor might utilize hidden strengths or untapped resources uncovered by exploring exceptions, or utilize knowledge of a client's strongly held preferred views to avoid generating resistance by making suggestions or proposing tasks that acknowledge and work within the preferred view.

The specific type of utilization discussed here goes a step further. In this chapter, we consider the possibility that even personality characteristics most counselors would view as negative might be put to work toward the solution. Some personality characteristics that counselors would like to change may be important to the client; they may be characteristics that clients feel make them who they are. When we respect this, the result is cooperation, rather than resistance.

There's an old joke that goes something like this:

Question: How do you tell a weed from a plant?
Answer: If you pull it out and it grows back, it's a weed. If you water it and it dies, it's a plant!

It's probably much more accurate to acknowledge that weeds and plants are not so easily distinguished, and that perhaps they are one and the same thing.

As Milton Erickson's idea of utilization is described in *In Search of Solutions,*

> ... the therapist should, like a good organic gardener, use every-thing that the client presented—even things that looked like weeds—as part of the therapy. The "weeds" of "resistance," symptoms, rigid beliefs, compulsive behavior, etc., were essen-tial components to be taken into consideration and actively used as part of the solution. (O'Hanlon and Weiner-Davis, 1989, pp. 15-16)

Clients seen as in denial are often thought to have a long list of problematic personality characteristics that counselors might come to appreciate as flowers rather than weeds. They are described as stubborn, defiant, manipulative, angry, and untrusting, or passive, disinterested, and uncaring. We usually view such characteristics as obstacles rather than aids to recovery. But is it ever possible to har-ness these forces to work in favor of the client?

To be sure, hanging a sign on stinkweed that says "rose" will not change the nature of the stinkweed. But that does not mean that we might not come to appreciate stinkweed for its unique ecological contributions (which include erosion control, creation of oxygen, and preservation of wetlands).

For example, if we consider the attributes of stubbornness and per-severance, our choice of words may depend as much on the intended goal of the person we are considering as on what the person is actu-ally doing. If we think it is a good goal, we may be more likely to call the attribute perseverance; if we disagree, stubbornness. If your client seems stubborn, consider whether the type of "sticking to one's guns" being displayed can be used to the client's benefit.

Likewise, if a client seems manipulative or defiant, have the client consider the possibility of using this independence and strong will as part of the solution. If you view your client as passive, consider whether a serene acceptance of things as they are might be part of a better future for the client.

CASE STUDY: "SHE RUINED MY LIFE!"

Shelby, a nineteen-year-old in residential treatment, had been complaining in several consecutive groups about a girl who "ruined her life" in eighth grade. The group members seemed tired of hearing about this after three weeks of trying to get Shelby to stop blaming all her misfortune on her childhood nemesis, Brittany, and accept responsibility for her current situation. But Shelby was like a broken record.

Shelby had seen herself as a member of the most popular and elite of the eighth-grade crowd. She had unselfishly taken Brittany under her wing when Brittany moved into town and helped her feel like a part of her clique. But according to Shelby, Brittany was very jealous of her. She made up lies about her that the other girls believed and stole all her friends. Since Brittany was from a relatively wealthy family, she reinforced her position as Shelby's replacement by buying expensive gifts for the other girls in the clique and taking all of them, except for Shelby, on outings. According to Shelby, Brittany mocked and abused her every chance she got. Brittany was so afraid that Shelby would someday regain her place as leader of the group that she never passed up an opportunity to put Shelby down. Shelby eventually became a very angry young woman and withdrew almost completely from the social scene to hang out with the "bad" kids.

GROUP LEADER: It sounds like this girl really hated you.

SHELBY: She did.

GROUP LEADER: And do you think she realizes how what she did to you has affected your entire life?

SHELBY: I doubt it. I hope she doesn't know, because I wouldn't want to give her the satisfaction.

GROUP LEADER: It sounds like you'd really like to pay her back for all she's done to you. Are you still in touch with her?

SHELBY: No. I heard she moved.

GROUP LEADER: What did you used to do that used to upset her the most?

SHELBY: Mostly she upset me. The only times I think I got back at her were when I pretended not to be upset.

GROUP LEADER: So making believe she didn't affect you got under her skin?

SHELBY: Yeah, but then that would make her try even harder, until I couldn't take it any more. Then I usually ran away and cried.

GROUP LEADER: Maybe it would help for us to come up with a way to *really* pay her back. Even though she'd never even know about it.

SHELBY: What do you mean?

GROUP LEADER: Well, it seems like the only times you got to her, even a little bit, is when you pretended she didn't matter. I was just thinking if it would pay her back if she *really* didn't matter.
    Even though you're not in touch, she sounds like the kind of person who would be rooting against you. She'd want you to be a broken down, druggie loser. She'd wish for you to mess up in the program.

SHELBY: Yeah, she would. I hate her so much.

GROUP LEADER: Well, if the only times you got to her were when she thought she couldn't get to you, I was thinking about how much it would really bother her if you really got things together and didn't even have to pretend that she didn't matter. If you could make it so she didn't matter for real, and you weren't even pretending. Just imagine how mad that would make her . . .

The group leader is attempting to utilize Shelby's negative feelings about Brittany to motivate her to create a better life for herself. It's hard to imagine that a person who would refuse to get her life together for her own benefit would be willing to do it to spite someone she used to know in eighth grade. But that group session did seem to turn the focus away from complaints about Brittany and at least temporarily motivate Shelby to consider things within her control that might improve her situation.

There's another old joke that makes a point about utilization:

> In the days of the Roman Empire, a Christian and a lion were in the Colosseum. By some miracle, the Christian was able to scale the wall. But just as amazingly, the lion was able to scale the wall as well.
>
> The lion chased the Christian throughout the city and was steadily gaining on him. They reached the edge of the city, and the lion followed the Christian into the woods. The Christian tried to dart behind trees and ran as fast as he could. But he could see that he was tiring much more quickly than the lion.
>
> Finally, in desperation, the Christian fell to his knees and prayed, "Lord, please make this lion into a Christian."
>
> At that very moment the lion dropped to its knees and prayed, "Lord, thank You for this meal."

I think the point of this story is that even if you could make a lion into a Christian, you still couldn't keep it from being a lion. God made lions to be lions, and lions eat other animals, including the occasional Christian.

When we try to turn lions into lambs, or pussycats into tigers, we are bound to generate resistance. It's not up to us, as counselors, to re-create clients in our own image, or to decide which personality characteristics our clients should value. It's up to us to honor the decisions of our clients.

How can we tell the weeds from the plants? How can we trust our observation that a client is manipulative and defiant, when the client sees it as independent and strong willed?

The most respectful course of action seems to be to take your direction from the client. If clients express interest in your assistance in "weeding" their gardens, you might most respectfully work for the transformation or extinction of the characteristic. If, on the other hand, the client has decided the characteristic is not one the client wants to change, the respectful thing to do would be to utilize the characteristic to help make changes the client does want.

Chapter 19

Paradoxical Interventions

A paradoxical intervention is designed to be surprising and contrary to client expectations (Cooper, 1995).

ADVOCATING FOR THE "NO PROBLEM" POINT OF VIEW

It is sometimes helpful to clients for the counselor to play devil's advocate and argue for the "wrong" side of the client's ambivalence. This type of "reverse psychology" is explained in *Motivational Interviewing* (Miller and Rollnick, 1991) as one that may evoke "statements of problem recognition, expressions of concern, intention to change, and optimism" (p. 86).

The same concept is addressed in *A Brief Guide to Brief Therapy* (Cade and O'Hanlon, 1993).

> When a therapist becomes too clearly identified with the arguments in favor of change, whether this position be explicitly or implicitly communicated, it is as though he or she colonizes those arguments, leaving available to the client or family members only the counter-arguments (or the "yes, buts") to that change . . .
>
> Conversely, when a therapist identifies with and validates the arguments in favor of caution or against change . . . family members are then left, as it were, with ownership of the counter-arguments . . . we are much more likely to be persuaded by self-generated arguments and counter-arguments than by the arguments of others.
>
> We use the term "colonization" deliberately in that, no matter how benevolent the colonizer, the process of colonization is one

of a lessening of self-determination and control over choices on the part of the colonized. (p. 156)

There is no need to use this technique in a sneaky, underhanded, or manipulative manner. Sharing your ideas about using this technique and what you hope to accomplish by it may make it even more effective, and demonstrates your respect for and trust in the client.

SYMPTOM PRESCRIPTION

Sometimes therapists will advise their clients to continue or even increase the symptoms they are trying to ameliorate so that clients who feel no control over their symptoms can take control. The conscious decision to intentionally increase problematic behavior is also called "escalation" (Cade and O'Hanlon, 1993).

The following case study illustrates the results of a successful application of this technique.

CASE STUDY: LEARNING TO LIE

Shirley, who was working in group therapy to overcome her dishonesty, had agreed to a homework assignment in a previous group that she at first thought was a joke: Tell one extra lie a day. She had explained that she "just couldn't help herself," and "lied for no good reason, just out of habit." Shirley often felt embarrassed when caught in her lies and said she wanted to change, but wasn't sure if she could break the habit, since she lied "without thinking."

She agreed to the assignment of telling one "extra" lie a day, as an experiment.

GROUP LEADER: So how did you do with your homework?

SHIRLEY: Terrible.

GROUP LEADER: Maybe it wasn't such a good assignment.

SHIRLEY: [Smiling] Yes, it was. That was just my one extra lie for today!

GROUP LEADER: So you got something out of the assignment?

SHIRLEY: Yes. A lot. To be honest, at first I thought this was the stupidest idea I ever heard—even after you explained what you were hoping might happen. I do lie a lot without even knowing it. But telling that *extra* lie, I had to really plan it. This made me more conscious of my lying, doing this extra lie on purpose. And I felt more stupid lying, even though some of my automatic lies are about just as stupid things.

GROUP LEADER: What else did you learn?

SHIRLEY: By telling that extra lie, I learned that I *can* control my lying. If I really had no control over my lying, I wouldn't be able to lie on purpose like that. And if I can have control to lie more, I can have control to lie less.

This assignment of symptom prescription succeeded in heightening the client's awareness of a behavior she wanted to change, and it helped her gain self-confidence that the change was within her power to accomplish. The group leader did not look upon the symptom prescription as an attempt to trick the client into changing. The group leader took care to explain the reasons for trying this paradoxical intervention and what might be accomplished, and left it up to the client to decide if it was worth a try as an experiment. Even though the client was skeptical about taking on the assignment, it was done with her fully informed consent and agreement.

Another type of symptom prescription may be helpful to anxious clients who are distracted by thoughts of something bad happening. Suggesting that the client try to bring on the feared event or condition may be helpful in either of two ways: (1) the client will be unable to bring on the feared event or condition, and so will be less anxious and distracted by the prospect; or (2) the client will succeed in bringing on the feared event or condition, and it will be over with. The client will have experience dealing with the feared event or condition, and realize that it wasn't really as bad as feared.

My favorite example of this type of symptom prescription is offered by Dr. David D. Burns (1999) in *The Feeling Good Handbook*. He tells of his success asking clients concerned about their sanity to "go crazy." If a client is highly anxious about keeping it together, Burns might say, "I know you've been afraid of cracking up for many years. This would be as good a time as any to go ahead and get it over with. After all, you are with a psychiatrist. Why don't you go ahead and do it? Please try your hardest to lose control and crack up" (p. 229).

Burns writes that he might even demonstrate bizarre behavior for the client, by standing on his desk and singing. He reports that most often clients laugh and feel relieved, realizing that if they can't crack up on purpose when they're trying to, there's not too much chance that they'll crack up by accident, and their anxiety about the matter is lessened.

PARADOXICAL PATTERN INTERVENTION

Some pattern intervention tasks that qualify as paradoxical are surprising to the client or out of the ordinary for a therapeutic setting. Sometimes simply suggesting a rearrangement of the sequence of events surrounding the problem can be helpful. For example, if a client has a pattern of not notifying his spouse when he's coming home late, and then drinking with his friends, coming home and acting obnoxiously, and profusely apologizing the next day to his wife, the counselor might suggest to the client that he apologize to his wife *before* going out drinking.

Chapter 20

Stop Trying So Hard

If you find yourself more upset at a lack of progress than your client, you may be trying too hard to be helpful. In some cases, the harder we work, the more our clients accept a passive role. When some clients get the feeling that we are accepting all the responsibility for continuing progress, they feel relieved of any responsibility for their own situations.

"In the prototypical case," write the authors of *Working with the Problem Drinker,*

> the therapist complains of having attempted numerous therapeutic interventions to which the client has neither complied nor responded. Usually, the therapist has reacted to this situation by working even harder at "helping" the client. The most common result of this is a series of increasingly complicated, creative, and/or aggressive-confrontational intervention tactics. Most often, continued failure has served to reinforce a vicious cycle in which the view of these clients as being difficult leads to increasingly aggressive treatment strategies, which, in turn, are resisted . . . (Berg and Miller, 1992, p. 29)

Other times, you may be trying too hard to explore sensitive issues, such as sexual or physical abuse, that your client is not ready to talk about, and you may be viewing the resistance you helped create as a treatment impasse. In these situations, it may be better to avoid a sense of urgency, go slow, and establish a firm foundation for change.

Still other times, your client may simply be at a plateau, or a natural resting place where clients need a rest from changing to consolidate recent gains. Review past progress with your client. Bring up the possibility that now may be a good time to stop and consolidate recent gains. Validate the accomplishments and recognize the *maintenance* of changes as a real accomplishment.

When your client is ready, ask the client to suggest some highly achievable goals. Think small. Then think even smaller. Trying too hard with clients in this situation may backfire on both of you.

FORGET ABOUT THE PROBLEM

Instead of a focus on stopping the problem, focus instead on starting the solution. Solution development processes can be completely independent of and unrelated to problem processes (Walter and Peller, 2000). That is to say, it is not necessary to fully understand a problem to help your clients create better lives. According to many practitioners and researchers, addressing the problem may even *be* the problem. In *Brief Therapy with Intimidating Cases,* the authors write,

> [W]e regard as central to our model that problems, however they may have started, *persist* because of the persistent tack the complainant has been taking in his or her efforts to resolve the complaint; we call this tack the *attempted solution.* This idea is the principal factor in our . . . model. Thus the thrust of therapy is not to get the complainants to *do* something so much as to *stop* what they have been doing about the problem. (italics in original, Fisch and Schlanger, 1999, p. 2)

FORGET ABOUT THE SOLUTION

Walter and Peller take this line of thinking one step further and advocate abandonment of working on solutions. Sometimes your client may just want someone to talk to. As they write in *Recreating Brief Therapy,* "we have decided to abandon the problem/solution distinction . . . our work focuses on the creative aspects of conversing" (Walter and Peller, 2000, p. 63). Some clients get all they want out of therapy by just having someone listen to them think out loud so they feel understood. Their counselors can be most helpful by listening to understand, rather than listening to change, the client.

HELP YOUR CLIENT TO STOP TRYING SO HARD

As noted previously, some practitioners theorize that many problems are kept alive by the clients' continuing attempts to solve them (Fisch and Schlanger, 1999; Fisch, Weakland, and Segal, 1982; Murphy and Duncan, 1997). As the authors of *The Tactics of Change* put it,

> We do not believe that persistence in inappropriate handling of difficulties must require either fundamental defects in family organization or mental deficits in the individual actors. Rather, we believe that people persist in actions that maintain problems inadvertently, and often with the best of intentions. Indeed, people may get caught in such repetitive behavior even when they are aware that what they are doing is not working. . . . (Fisch, Weakland, and Segal, 1982, pp. 15-16)

Or, as Moms Mabley more succinctly put it, "If you always do what you always did, you'll always get what you always got!" (quoted in Hayes, Strosahl, and Wilson, 1999, p. 235).

Some problems seem to disappear on their own once a client gives up on a "solution" that is not working. In these cases, an intervention that interrupts the attempted solution may be successful. In the following case study, parents find out, by accident, that their attempts to cheer up their daughter were a major ingredient in her depression.

CASE STUDY: LOOKING ON THE BRIGHT SIDE

The parents of Linda are a good example. They tried, very hard, to have pleasant discussions with their daughter. But Linda was even more withdrawn and sad during family visits than she was at most other times. Her parents were trying their best to address this problem, but it kept getting worse.

Linda felt misunderstood by her family, and the more her parents tried to cheer her up, the more depressed she became. It seems as if her parents' sincere and caring efforts to cheer her up had given her the impression that they didn't understand the depths of her despair. And this made her even sadder. But the parents kept trying harder with a strategy that wasn't working. The more they told Linda to look on the bright side, the more withdrawn she became.

Whenever Linda tried to talk about things that were upsetting to her, her parents tried to protect her from her sad feelings, and turned the conversation to things they considered more positive. They insisted on pointing out the things they thought Linda had to be thankful for.

Luckily for everyone, the dad finally ran out of patience. He'd been having financial and marital problems, and he couldn't hide his frustration any longer. He told his daughter that maybe she was right for being so pessimistic and that, no matter how hard he tried to be a good dad, it was never good enough. He told her he agreed that the entire family led pitiful lives.

Instead of being upset, Linda sympathized with her dad. She explained that he was feeling a lot like she had been feeling: she would never get out of treatment, and even if she did, nothing would be different. The family seemed to have more substantive conversations from that point on. They shared their disappointments, and Linda's parents gave her a chance to speak, in depth, about the reasons she was so sad.

By trying so hard to cheer Linda up, the parents had been short-circuiting almost any meaningful conversation. But when they stopped trying so hard to cheer her up, the problems of communicating with their daughter virtually disappeared.

Take a close look at the therapeutic impasse. If your client has been trying too hard with an old solution, or looking too hard for a new solution, consider the possibility that simply abandoning the failing attempted solutions might break the impasse.

Chapter 21

Other Techniques

SELF-DISCLOSURE

Some practitioners and treatment programs have very strict rules regarding self-disclosure. Avoiding inappropriate relationships is, of course, the highest priority, and a cornerstone of every ethical code for counselors. That said, not all personal information that counselors share with clients violates the sanctity of the client-counselor relationship. Properly timed and appropriate self-disclosure can sometimes move a stuck client, especially when used by counselors who do not generally share anything personal.

Of course, any self-disclosure on the part of counselors must have a client-benefiting reason behind it. Self-disclosure should be viewed as a possible tool for meeting client needs, not your own.

One client-benefiting reason is to help the client be comfortable with your level of training and experience. Self-disclosure may also allow you and your client to examine a process that is not working (Littrell, 1998). By honestly sharing your own feelings about your perceived lack of progress with the client, you might provide your client the opportunity to get "unstuck."

Self-disclosures similar to the following have had varied results, but sometimes succeeded by eliciting the client's previously unknown theory of change, by discovering that the client is seeing and can identify more progress than the counselor, or by eliciting client suggestions for improving the client-counselor relationship.

I'm feeling very inadequate as your counselor, and it worries me because if I'm not optimistic about your situation, I'm afraid this will rub off on you. I'm wondering if I can be doing anything differently than I have been, to be more helpful to you. I feel very badly about not being very helpful so far, and I need to know your thoughts on what I can do to improve our relationship.

Self-disclosures similar to the one above seem to encourage clients to share their ideas more often than regular periodic requests to review progress do. You might review with your client the tools you have been using unsuccessfully in treatment, and ask for the clients' opinions on what has and hasn't been helpful so far.

Other client-benefiting reasons for self-disclosure include modeling, normalizing, or validating one possibility for appropriate behavior, feelings, or perspectives. With clients who are really down on themselves, self-disclosures about mistakes you have made, similar to ones clients are concerned about, can sometimes be helpful. Clients may also benefit from self-disclosures they perceive as expressions of empathy (Hubble, Duncan, and Miller, 1999).

Finally, your self-disclosure might encourage your clients to share their theories of change and become partners in the therapeutic process.

WRITE YOUR CLIENT A LETTER

Simply presenting information in an unusual way can make an impression on your client. Writing a letter to your client and presenting it during a session can make the session and the information in the letter more memorable to your client. You might even combine this technique with the type of self-disclosure suggested previously.

Letters mailed to clients who may not keep the next (or even first!) appointment, or who have missed an appointment, can sometimes make a difference. This is especially true for those times when we think of just the right thing to say—after the client has left the session. These "letters of invitation" are fully discussed in *Narrative Means to Therapeutic Ends* (White and Epston, 1990).

The same text recommends use of "counter-referral letters" and "letters of reference" which report to the referring party or "to whom it may concern" on the progress a client has made. These letters may also include how thankful the therapist is for the opportunity to work with the client. Such letters may work to underscore client strengths, restore hope, and get the therapeutic process moving after a logjam.

HEALING RITUALS AND VISUALIZATIONS

Although they have no curative powers in and of themselves, healing rituals or visualizations may be helpful at certain points in the course of treatment of some clients. They could inspire hope and a positive expectation for change, and provide an emotional experience that encourages clients to mobilize their resources.

As noted in the self-help guide *Changing for Good,*

> *Emotional arousal* parallels consciousness-raising, but works on a deeper, feeling level and is equally important in the early stages of change. Known also as *dramatic release*—or, more traditionally, *catharsis*—emotional arousal is a significant, often sudden emotional experience related to the problem at hand. It is an extremely powerful process. (Prochaska, Norcross, and DiClemente, 1994, p. 28)

Healing Rituals

It's important to avoid the impression that the ceremony will perform some "magic" and essential that the client is fully on board as to the goal of the ritual and the rationale for how the ritual may achieve this goal. Rituals designed by the client are often the most effective. If a drawing or some other object can be represented as an externalization of the problem, a ritual disposing of it once and for all is often helpful.

In *The New Language of Change,* Insoo Kim Berg and Steve De Shazer recount a client-suggested ritual that was especially helpful. An eight-year-old girl was brought to treatment after being molested by a stranger in a shopping mall. They used a graphic scaling technique and asked the girl to draw an "x" on the line that showed how far she had come in therapy. Then they asked her for an idea on how to make that "x" go all the way to the top of the line, so she could put this incident behind her.

> After several minutes, during which time she shifted her weight from one foot to the other, she hit upon an idea and said, "I know what!" "What?" asked the therapist. The little girl replied in a rather somber voice, "We will burn the clothes I was wearing when it happened." The therapist, amazed at this creative idea, said, "That's a wonderful idea!" Soon after this session the child

and her parents had a ritual burning and then went out to dinner in a fancy restaurant to mark the end of therapy. (Berg and De Shazer, 1993, p. 23)

Visualizations

If your client is willing to try, visualizations may cause an emotional arousal that motivates change or provides a chance to learn things that might not have been learned otherwise. Speak at a pace and in a tone of voice that helps the client relax. Clients are generally asked to close their eyes. Except for those counselors most fluent in the technique, reading verbatim from a printed page is usually more helpful than "winging it."

You will be able to tell by the expressions on your clients' faces how they are reacting to the images they are picturing in their heads. One visualization that has been helpful to some clients is recounted here.

Close your eyes and relax. Imagine you're going on a trip, a journey. You're at the bottom of a big mountain, and you'd like to get to the top. You know that the view from the top of the mountain is going to be much more beautiful than the view from where you are now.

You look at your luggage, and you realize you'll never make it to the top of the mountain if you have to carry all that baggage. So you open the trunk, and take out the things you really don't need; things that will only hold you back. Imagine each of these things as you unpack them from your suitcase to leave them behind.

You look back up at the mountain, and realize that there are some things that you really *do* need to take on your trip. See yourself packing each of these essentials into a knapsack. You are ready to begin your climb.

It's hard at first. You get a few scrapes because you're not too used to climbing. But you begin to appreciate the beauty of the trail. It's a very beautiful trail. See yourself looking down to the bottom of the mountain, to where you used to be. You are pleasantly surprised with how far you've come. You notice that the bottom of the mountain looks different from your new vantage point.

Although you still have a long way to go, you're proud of what you've accomplished so far. Your journey begins to be easier, as you make more progress along the winding trail each day. See yourself moving more quickly along the path, no longer out of breath. Your excitement is building as you approach the top of the mountain.

You're there. You're at the top of the mountain. It's just as beautiful as you thought it would be. Everyone you love is with you to celebrate your achievement. Enjoy the celebration. . . .

When you are ready, open your eyes.

The "excess baggage" some clients imagine will be problematic personality traits, childhood traumas, or a lack of hope (this may be helpful in problem identification or clarification). The knapsack contents might include positive things clients want in their lives (which may be helpful to define goals).

Clients are often eager to talk about their visualization experience. For some it may be an emotional experience that impacts their current situation enough to help them back on track.

ART THERAPY

Even for inexperienced counselors with the best of intentions, art therapy techniques require experienced supervision. Even the most experienced art therapists sometimes find themselves in over their heads, having unleashed emotions they have difficulty handling.

Other therapists without a solid background in art therapy succumb to the temptation to misuse a client's artwork, as they provide convoluted explanations of the art that support the counselors' preexisting opinions about the case.

The art experience should be confirming and validating for clients—not necessarily for counselors and their preexisting viewpoints. It's important to hear what meaning the work has to our clients before we offer any suggestions or input.

As noted in *The New Language of Change,*

> Expressive arts therapy . . . calls for an atmosphere of mutual respect and expression, a non-judgmental attitude with regard to artistic productions, and a facilitative intent, rather than a critical or interpretive approach. (Friedman, 1993, p. 191)

Art, even outside therapy, is an emotional outlet that promotes self-awareness and personal growth (Rosenthal, 1998, pp. 78-79). It could be a way to reach clients who are unreachable otherwise. Through their artwork, clients may communicate things they might not communicate any other way.

Artwork can provide insight into clients' interests, abilities, and concerns. It may provide counselors with insight into how the client views the problem and help identify client resources that may be mobilized to combat the problem. Art activities can help build trust, enhance communication, and strengthen the therapeutic relationship.

Abstract art that represents depression, fears, or childhood abuse can be cathartic. Drawing pictures of a problem is one way to externalize it, and the picture may also be useful in the type of healing rituals we have already discussed.

ROLE-PLAYING

Experiential and action-oriented therapists make regular use of empty chairs to facilitate role-playing. This may be helpful to other therapists, as a departure from what they usually do (and what their clients have come to expect). To raise awareness of the perspective of others, to reduce polarization, and to help clients understand how others involved in the problem feel, the client is asked to change chairs and role-play each participant in a discussion.

The hope is not only for greater understanding of, for example, a spouse, but to move the client from *talking* about the spouse's problems to actually *experiencing* them. Rather than talk about a spouse, the client is invited to *be* the spouse. When a lack of insight into the feelings of another is the main obstacle, this technique may "unstick" a stuck client.

Another possibly helpful role-playing technique is role reversal. It involves physically changing places with the client and asking the client to role-play you, while you role-play the client. This provides clients with the opportunity to offer their perspective of your counseling approach. It also offers the counselor a unique opportunity to communicate with the client.

Role reversals can also provide an opportunity for clients to communicate about issues too painful to discuss in any other way. If the counselor, role-playing the client, answers questions by saying, "I don't know," the client, acting as the counselor, may build answers into the questions, or provide feedback on the counselor's therapeutic approach.

Successful use of this technique might look something like this:

CLIENT (AS COUNSELOR): So why are you so angry all the time?

COUNSELOR (AS CLIENT): I don't know.

CLIENT (AS COUNSELOR): Do you really not know, or are you just afraid that if you tell me I will judge you?

COUNSELOR (AS CLIENT): I DON'T KNOW.

CLIENT (AS COUNSELOR): Is it something from your childhood? Something you're ashamed about? Something really bad you don't like to talk about?

COUNSELOR (AS CLIENT): I don't want to talk about it.

CLIENT (AS COUNSELOR): I understand. If you are not ready to talk about something now, I will wait until you are ready.

This brief exchange seems to support three educated guesses about this client: (1) the client is afraid of being judged; (2) the client has had childhood experiences that are affecting the client in the present; and (3) the client is not quite ready to share all the details of these experiences and would appreciate the counselor's patience.

Role reversal may provide valuable feedback on your personal counseling style and choice of techniques, especially as they relate to a specific client. There is a possibility that role reversal will make just enough of a difference in the client's comfort level to facilitate discussion of sensitive topics the client is reluctant to talk about otherwise. In the best of all possible outcomes, the client will actually share, in the questions while posing as counselor, important details that the counselor can utilize to break a treatment impasse.

Another twist on the role-playing technique is a favorite of William Weikel. He suggests the use of his "telephone" technique in group settings, for clients with unresolved issues with parents.

> The client, after discussing an issue that remains unresolved and is troublesome . . . is given a telephone that is not wired or asked to use an imaginary telephone to call the person with whom the client has unresolved feelings. With help from the therapist and/or group members, a dialogue begins. The client can put the other party on "hold" to gain advice or direction from the group in order to role-play a conversation or try alternative approaches. (Weikel, 1998, p. 189)

This technique may allow clients to process their feelings and move some toward closure of "unfinished business."

The techniques offered in this section are just a few of the many creative techniques used by experienced counselors. When trying them for the first time, counselors may want to explain them in advance to clients and frame the exercise as an experiment. Your own comfort level will probably be a reliable gauge of when to use these techniques.

We often encourage our clients to take reasonable risks, and our use of counseling techniques could model reasonable risk taking for them. When things don't go as well as we'd like, we can also model handling the "failure" of any technique, by accepting responsibility and using it as an opportunity to learn.

SECTION V:
QUESTIONS AND ANSWERS

Chapter 22

Practical Concerns

Q: One of the most difficult things for me is dealing with the client who answers every question with "I don't know" or just gives a yes or no answer. How can you get such a person to talk?

A: Closed-ended questions—the kind that can be answered just yes or no—are not usually the best kind to ask your clients. Open-ended questions or requests for additional information necessarily require more extended responses.

For example, "Tell me about your family" is likely to generate more discussion than, "Do you have any brothers or sisters?" or "Do you love your parents?" More information on using open-ended questions is available in *Motivational Interviewing* (Miller and Rollnick, 1991).

If clients have been mandated, they may be thinking that anything they say could be used against them. Section III offers some suggestions for these situations.

Also consider the possibility that your client really may not know the answers to the questions you are asking. In these cases, a suggestion such as, "Well, let's put our heads together and see if we can figure it out" might help. Showing a genuine interest in what your clients have to say seems to be among the best ways to get clients to communicate with you.

Q: I've tried the normalizing idea. There are just some clients who don't want to be normal. If they find out that nothing is wrong with them, they're very disappointed. How do you deal with them?

A: Finding out "what's wrong" is very important to some clients. In these cases, validation seems to work better than normalization. Their theory of change often involves identifying a root cause, which will help them understand and explain their current difficulties. This in turn is expected to help them to avoid repeating past mistakes.

Trying to normalize or talk these clients out of their problems may generate resistance. Keep in mind that if we minimize the seriousness of the situation of clients in emotional pain, we might make their situation even more painful. Clients react to our attempts to normalize as they would to any other challenge to their preferred view. In these cases, empathizing with clients, validating clients, and a willingness to work within the client's theory of change is what seems to be most helpful.

> **Q:** My experience has been that once clients have bottomed out, they are open to almost any intervention, and almost any intervention is helpful. But before they have bottomed out, there is very little you can do. Isn't the best time to use almost any technique when alcoholics and addicts have hit bottom?

A: Being in a very painful situation motivates some clients to accept our suggestions. But others seem almost paralyzed by their pain.

Chiauzzi (1991) warns against an assumption that more pain makes for better outcomes.

> The "hitting bottom" concept . . . assumes that pain has a linear relationship with success: the more the better. However, many alcoholics and addicts are in a high degree of pain at the outset and some use substances to medicate this pain. An increase in pain often immobilizes them to the point of hopelessness. (p. 17)

The idea of waiting to offer our help until we feel that the client is in the "right amount" of pain does not seem very ethical. Should we dismiss a group of potential clients in the hopes that the terrible things we expect to happen to them will make them more open to our advice? That would be like a doctor withholding advice from a junk-food-eating, cigarette-smoking, overweight couch potato until *after* a heart attack.

Those of us in the helping professions have an obligation to try and help our clients avoid any deeper bottoms than they've already experienced.

> **Q:** Your text offers few techniques, if any, which could be considered confrontational. Have you totally dismissed confrontation as a useful tool?

A: No. My opposition is to heavy confrontation as the *only* tool. As noted in the previous answer, emotional pain does not seem to have a direct relationship with successful outcome.

Perhaps the mixed results from confrontational techniques can be explained by the theory (Chiauzzi, 1991) that there's an optimal level of discomfort: uncomfortable enough to motivate change, but not so uncomfortable the client can't think straight. Perhaps confrontation is more suitable for "low pain" clients for whom the additional discomfort may be motivational. In "high pain" or already hopeless clients, heavily confrontational, in-your-face techniques intended to drive home "what's wrong" may destroy motivation.

> **Q:** Your discussion of the creation of resistance points an accusing finger of blame at counselors who insist on their "own agenda." Don't we pay counselors to know more about life and addiction than their clients?

A: I'm not comfortable with the balance of power in some counseling relationships. I'm speaking of the very small minority of cases where counselors consider themselves the experts. These counselors see clients as having problems the clients don't understand—or may not even be aware of—so the counselors are willing to accept responsibility for deciding what type of life is best for their clients.

In other counseling relationships, almost always where the client has been mandated to treatment or is an involuntary client, clients see themselves as experts. They see their counselors as not knowing about the "real" world and as nuisances that they must put up with.

My view is that clients and counselors are both experts, and each should be respected for their very different areas of expertise. Clients are experts on what they are and are not willing to do at any point in their treatment. They have a wealth of experiences that counselors could never know about until clients tell them. Clients are also the experts on what treatment goals they are willing to embrace and reject, and what has and hasn't worked for them in the past.

Counselors are experts in helping people change. They have a willingness to put their training and experience to work on behalf of their clients.

It is clients' willingness to share their expertise that gives meaning and value to the counselor's expertise; unless clients share their expertise, the counselors' training and experience can be of little benefit. Denying or devaluing clients' expertise may lead to resistance.

The most effective counseling relationships are based on mutual respect, and both client and counselor show a willingness to benefit from the other's expertise.

> **Q:** When you discuss treatment readiness, are you really talking about awareness? For example, how aware are clients of themselves, their conditioning, and their preferred (positive and self-defeating) patterns of behavior and choosing? And how aware is the therapist of these same things? Isn't readiness mostly a function of awareness?

A: Perhaps. The problem arises when counselors see themselves as the keepers of "the truth" and clients with differing opinions as "lacking in awareness." This is not conducive to the mutually respectful relationship discussed in the previous question. In a mutually respectful relationship, clients and counselors help raise each other's level of awareness.

> **Q:** I agree that setting positive goals is important, but isn't abstinence really a negative goal (*don't* use)? Would you suggest we do away with this as a long-term goal?

A: Of course not. The point is that a focus on abstinence to the exclusion of positive goals often makes abstinence more difficult. There are also many positively stated goals that may be problematic for the same reason: they remind the addict of the problem. (For example, "I will drink only nonalcoholic beer.")

Recovering people can maintain abstinence and still have their problem occupy center stage—even after years of successfully avoiding alcohol and drugs. Strangely, their relationship with drugs or alcohol may still distract them from more rewarding pursuits, as they spend as much time or more thinking about not using as they used to spend using. The most helpful positively stated goals often have nothing at all to do with drinking or drug use.

> **Q:** You seem to be saying that identifying the root cause of a problem is not helpful or, worse yet, a waste of time. How can a counselor be helpful in a theoretical vacuum? Isn't the identification of "why" important to avoid future relapse?

A: There is one great weakness in all the backward-looking strategies that call for identification of the root cause of the problem. That weakness is the likelihood that a person can never know for certain why he or she has any problem, including addiction. Counselors' explanations often reveal more about the counselor than about the true cause of the client's difficulty.

For example, consider the problem of depression. Psychodynamic explanations often see the problem as rooted in early childhood experiences, but a psychiatrist using a medical model will likely see the cause as a chemical imbalance in the brain. Some counselors may feel the condition is hereditary, with a defective gene as a major contributing factor. A fundamentalist Christian counselor might frame the problem, as well as the solution, in terms of openness to the Holy Spirit. A cognitive therapist might see the cause as inappropriate or distorted thoughts. A solution-focused therapist might explain that the problem is being maintained by a problem focus, which has resulted in a failure to identify and harness available resources. A therapist with a feminist orientation might consider the environmental and cultural setting of a male-dominated society as an important contributing factor, and so on.

Each explanation reveals more about the theories of the counselor than the realities of the cause or causes of the client's depression. And none of these explanations, however helpful in some individual cases, can be guaranteed to be helpful in solving the problem. Each of these explanations has resulted in highly successful outcomes for some; and has been a dismal failure for others.

If you're lost, you could spend all your time figuring out where you've been and how you got where you are. Or you could, instead, try to figure out how to get where you want to be. Our suggestion is that in some cases, especially when identification of the root cause is not a priority of the client, it makes more sense to devote a bigger portion of your time to figuring out how to get clients where they want to be, rather than helping them raise their awareness of how they got where they are. Many times, a heightened awareness of the problem will be the *result* of change, rather than the cause.

> **Q:** Looking toward the future is fine. But a counselor's job is to tell it like it is—not to encourage false hopes. What about the clients that can't reasonably expect to have a good future?

A: There's a difference between building hope and encouraging wishful thinking. Wishful thinking is passive and requires no planning or active role for the client. Wishing for a fairy godmother to come along and wave a wand and make everything better is an extreme example of wishful thinking.

Building hope, on the other hand, is an active process, with clients fully engaged in the planning and taking an active role in their own futures. Hope, as we speak of it here, involves a realistic expectation that wishful thinking does not. Counselors can be helpful to their clients by understanding this difference, and working to build a realistic hope in a better future.

> **Q:** Your discussion of externalization is very interesting, but what are the implications for most self-help groups, in which participants typically begin by saying, "I am an alcoholic" or "I am an addict." Are you suggesting that this practice may be harmful?

A: To some counselors, the externalization, "I have a problem with alcohol, but I'm *not* an alcoholic" is seen as an attempt by clients to avoid being held accountable—an attempt to get off the hook and refuse responsibility for their drinking or drug use. The concept of externalization is controversial, because many in the addiction field believe that the admission, "I am an alcoholic" or "I am an addict" is part of a necessary First Step toward recovery. People for whom this statement *was* the first step in their recovery often feel that recovery would have been impossible without it. The success of self-help groups is well documented, and certainly needs no defense from me.

Our suggestion is that in some cases a client statement such as, "I am an alcoholic" or "I am an addict" is the type of internalization that makes changing much harder. Clients then may feel *less* accountable, since they have a lifelong condition that will never change. They may feel as if they can't help being who they really are. Changing the "I am a problem" statements to "I have a relationship with the problem" statements may make these people more accountable.

Externalization of a drinking or drug problem allows clients to imagine themselves free of the problem. Internalizing the idea that they'll always be alcoholics or addicts robs clients of that future option. With the statement, "I am an alcoholic," the counseling question becomes, "What can we do to deal with this fact?" The focus is on something that is unchangeable. The response may be more reactive, with the problem staying at center stage—even after years of abstinence.

With the statement, "I have a drinking problem," the counseling question is more likely to become "How can we solve this problem?" The response may be more proactive, and so the focus is more likely to become a happier and more rewarding life.

Chapter 23

Ethical Concerns

Q: Is it ethical to pretend to agree with clients when you really don't? Aren't a lot of these techniques manipulative? How can we ask our clients to be honest and straightforward when we ourselves are playing these types of head games?

A: I believe that the therapeutic techniques presented in this book, when used appropriately, are among the most ethical counseling tools. They incorporate respect for clients, respect for the clients' points of view, and acknowledgment that clients do and should have the last word on how they wish to live their lives.

The best way to avoid many ethical problems is to explain to your client exactly what you are doing. Let the client in on your thinking, your use of the technique, and the result you are hoping to accomplish. For example, rather than pretend that you totally agree with your client's preferred view, you might say, "I'm not sure that I see things exactly as you do. But I respect your opinion and have learned through experience that I am often more helpful when I accept, rather than challenge, a client's view of things. So I am very willing to work with you on that basis."

Or you might explain to your clients, in a closing summary, how you were trying to be helpful by using hope-inspiring reflections that included possibilities not present in their original statements, and ask them if they noticed, or if they feel any more hopeful than they did at the beginning of the session.

None of the suggested techniques are any less effective when fully explained to clients, and the explanation often helps build trust and a sense of true collaboration—which make the techniques more effective than they would have been otherwise. All of the techniques are presented as possibilities for some clients some of the time, and are best used in combination with (rather than instead of) your other preferred techniques.

> **Q:** The techniques you suggest might improve a client's outlook—without really improving the situation. Aren't some of the "improvements" you talk about mostly placebo effects?

A: Building hope and the expectation of success in psychotherapy is not the same as giving a sugar pill to a terminally ill patient. In medical research, placebos are used to help measure "real" improvement versus "psychological" improvement. When psychological improvement is the "real" thing you are measuring, the idea of placebo is not very useful.

This question acknowledges that clients may leave in the same set of circumstances as they entered, with the only major difference being that they are happier and feel more confident that they can deal with their problems on their own. This answer acknowledges the same possibility, but considers that to be a very satisfactory outcome.

The best therapeutic techniques, like the best medicines, tap into human beings' innate ability to heal themselves.

> **Q:** Especially with the reframing and utilization techniques, you seem to be saying that to be good counselors we must forfeit our rights to have any opinions of what is right or wrong, or good or bad. Shouldn't we be trying to replace unhealthy values with healthy ones? Isn't that the only way to prevent relapse and assure long-term, quality sobriety? How can we, in good conscience, condone client behaviors we know in our hearts are wrong?

A: Most of what we think about and say to our clients is shaped by our own personal values. It is doubtful that avoiding this is possible and even less certain that it would be advisable even if possible. But our clients often come to us at very vulnerable points in their lives. They may be quite open to the idea of the counselor as a guru, who has all the answers and will show them how to best lead their lives. But it would be unethical to use our positions as counselors to promote our own personal values.

An ideal recovery program will include opportunities for development of values and spiritual growth that are outside the primary counseling relationship. Personal growth and the development of values is a natural by-product of successful therapy. However, the ideal counselor is a neutral observer, who doesn't impose his or her personal values on clients.

The reframing and utilization techniques can be useful in helping clients, while avoiding the temptation to remake clients in our own image. They are appropriate tools for some situations where the best way to be helpful is to respect, rather than challenge, the client's worldview.

Being a helpful counselor in no way requires renunciation of your membership in the human race. You certainly wouldn't reframe an ax murderer's behavior as "population control" or dismiss him with an attempt at utilization such as, "Why don't you just become a lumberjack and use your devotion to chopping things up for good instead of evil"!

Chapter 24

In Closing

Q: This text focuses on counseling techniques. Do you mean to imply that the burden of responsibility for change is on the counselor? Could you summarize your idea of the ideal counseling relationship?

A: Since this is a book for counselors and not clients, I have left out all the many suggestions I might have for clients to be more successful at changing. Counselors are the audience, and I have left out what others outside that audience (clients, family members, society) might do to be helpful.

Recent research (Hubble, Duncan, and Miller, 1999) seems to suggest that much of what is helpful to clients is outside the realm of any specific therapeutic technique or approach. That is to say, factors common to most therapy (empathy, warmth, acceptance, encouragement of risk taking) and extratherapeutic change (client characteristics and environmental factors) may account for 70 percent of treatment outcome. So the idea that the clients' failure to get what they want is the sole responsibility of the counselor is clearly unfair.

What seems to be important about our techniques is that the counselor and client both expect them to be helpful. This means that a willingness to see the benefits of the widest range of therapeutic interventions may be most helpful to our clients. It's not about blaming either counselors or clients for less than successful outcomes.

As put in *Psychotherapy with "Impossible" Cases,*

> In any retrospective analysis . . . it is tempting to create straw men. If only the therapist were smarter, more astute, or "theoretically correct," then the impossible case would never have evolved. Likewise, if the client was more open-minded, compli-

ant, or healthy, then a good outcome would be assured. These assertions are useless. "Shoot the therapist" or "shoot the client" are misdirected pastimes. (Duncan, Hubble, and Miller, 1997, p. 13)

An appreciation for the unique talents and strengths of each client seems to contribute to successful outcomes. As Steven Friedman (1993) observes,

To see people in terms of pathology or to see them in terms of competence is a matter of choice rather than truth. We choose to view our clients as competent, while acknowledging that the patterns of behaving and thinking in which they have become caught may have hidden their competence. (p. 108)

If there is a common thread that runs through all the interventions in this text it is, above all, respect for the client. That client has the complete responsibility for making any changes, and that is as it should be. Counselors are responsible for their level of helpfulness to the client's efforts.

A unifying theme of this text has been the encouragement of an individualized approach for each client.

Several studies have come to the questionable conclusion that techniques don't matter, because success rates are about the same for many different approaches. These studies may be set up, for example, with 100 clients in twelve-step treatment, 100 clients in cognitive therapy, and 100 clients in brief therapy.

When each approach succeeds with about one-third of the clients, an assumption is made that the approaches are comparably successful, and it makes little difference to clients which form of treatment they attend. But suppose each of these approaches helps a *different* third of the clients, or that there are at least some clients who failed with one approach that might have benefited from a competing approach.

Addicts may be as different from one another as they are from nonaddicts. So knowing what works or doesn't work for one client may not help us as much as we might hope with our next client. No single technique or approach will be as helpful to our clients as a willingness to keep trying—beyond what our most favored approach has to offer.

Bibliography

American Psychiatric Association (1994). *Diagnostic and statistical manual of mental disorders,* Fourth edition, American Psychiatric Association (Washington, DC).

Berg, Insoo Kim (1994). *Family based services,* W. W. Norton and Co. (New York).

Berg, Insoo Kim and De Shazer, Steve (1993). Making numbers talk: Language in therapy. In Steve Friedman (ed.), *The new language of change* (pp. 5-24). Guilford Press (New York).

Berg, Insoo Kim and Miller, Scott D. (1992). *Working with the problem drinker,* W.W. Norton and Co. (New York).

Berg, Insoo Kim and Reuss, Norman H. (1998). *Solutions step by step,* W. W. Norton and Co. (New York).

Bertolino, Bob and O'Hanlon, Bill (1999). *Invitation to possibility-land,* Brunner/Mazel (Philadelphia).

Budman, Simon H., ed. (1981). *Forms of brief therapy,* Guilford Press (New York).

Burns, David D. (1999). *The feeling good handbook,* Plume/Penguin Books (New York).

Cade, Brian and O'Hanlon, William H. (1993). *A brief guide to brief therapy,* W. W. Norton and Co. (New York).

Chiauzzi, Emil J. (1991). *Preventing relapse in the addictions,* Pergamon Press (New York).

Cooper, John F. (1995). *A primer of brief psychotherapy,* W. W. Norton and Co. (New York).

Davidson, Robin, Rollnick, Stephen, and MacEwan, Ian, eds. (1991). *Counseling problem drinkers.* Routledge (London).

Dolnick, Edward (1998). *Madness on the couch,* Simon and Schuster (New York).

Duncan, Barry L., Hubble, Mark A., and Miller, Scott D. (1997). *Psychotherapy with "impossible" cases,* W. W. Norton and Co. (New York).

Duncan, Barry L. and Miller, Scott D. (2000). *The heroic client,* Jossey-Bass (San Francisco).

Ecker, Bruce and Hulley, Laurel (1996). *Depth oriented brief therapy,* Jossey-Bass Publishers (San Francisco).

Edelwich, Jerry and Brodsky, Archie (1992). *Group counseling for the resistant client,* Lexington Books (New York).

Eron, Joseph B. and Lund, Thomas W. (1996). *Narrative solutions in brief therapy*, Guilford Press (New York).

Fisch, Richard and Schlanger, Karin (1999). *Brief therapy with intimidating cases*, Jossey-Bass Publishers (San Francisco).

Fisch, Richard, Weakland, John H., and Segal, Lynn (1982). *The tactics of change*, Jossey-Bass Publishers (San Francisco).

Freedman, Jill and Combs, Gene (1996). *Narrative therapy*, W. W. Norton and Co. (New York).

Friedman, Steve, ed. (1993). *The new language of change*, Guilford Press (New York).

Furman, Ben and Ahola, Tapani (1992). *Solution talk*, W. W. Norton and Co. (New York).

Goldstein, Eda G. and Noonan, Maryellen (1999). *Short term treatment and social work practice*, The Free Press (New York).

Gorski, Terence T. (1996). *Brief strategic problem-solving group therapy*, Herald House/Independence Press (Independence, MO).

Hayes, Steven C., Strosahl, Kirk D., and Wilson, Kelly G. (1999). *Acceptance and commitment therapy*, Guilford Press (New York).

Hopps, June Gary, and Pinderhughes, Elain (1999). *Group work with overwhelmed clients*, The Free Press (New York).

Hubble, Mark A., Duncan, Barry L., and Miller, Scott D. (1999). *The heart and soul of change*, American Psychological Association (Washington, DC).

Hudson, Pat (1996). *The solution focused woman*, W. W. Norton and Co. (New York).

Janis, Irving L. (1983). *Short term counseling*, Yale University Press (New Haven).

Lazarus, Arnold A. (1997). *Brief but comprehensive psychotherapy*, Springer Publishing Co. (New York).

Littrell, John M. (1998). *Brief counseling in action*, W. W. Norton and Co. (New York).

Marlatt, G. Alan (1998). *Harm reduction*, Guilford Press (New York).

McFarland, Barbara (1995). *Brief therapy and eating disorders*, Jossey-Bass Publishers (San Francisco).

Metcalf, Linda (1998). *Solution focused group therapy*, The Free Press (New York).

Miller, Scott D. and Berg, Insoo Kim (1995). *The miracle method*, W. W. Norton and Co. (New York).

Miller, Scott D., Hubble, Mark A., and Duncan, Barry L., eds. (1996). *Handbook of solution focused brief therapy*, Jossey-Bass Publishers (San Francisco).

Miller, Scott D., Hubble, Mark A., and Duncan, Barry L. (1997). *Escape from Babel*, W. W. Norton and Co. (New York).

Miller, William R. and Rollnick, Stephen (1991). *Motivational interviewing*, Guilford Press (New York).

Murphy, John J. and Duncan, Barry L. (1997). *Brief intervention for school problems,* Guilford Press (New York).

O'Connell, Bill (1998). *Solution-focused therapy,* Sage Publications (London).

O'Hanlon, Bill and Beadle, Sandy (1997). *Guide to possibility land,* W. W. Norton and Co. (New York).

O'Hanlon, Bill and Hudson, Pat (1995). *Stop blaming start loving!,* W. W. Norton and Co. (New York).

O'Hanlon, Patricia Hudson and O'Hanlon, William Hudson (1991). *Rewriting love stories,* W. W. Norton and Co. (New York).

O'Hanlon, William Hudson and Weiner-Davis, Michelle (1989). *In search of solutions,* W. W. Norton and Co. (New York).

Omer, Haim (1994). *Critical interventions in psychotherapy,* W. W. Norton and Co. (New York).

Peele, Stanton (1995). *Diseasing of America,* Jossey-Bass Publishers (San Francisco).

Prochaska, James O., Norcross, John C., and DiClemente, Carlo C. (1994). *Changing for good,* William Morrow (New York).

Rosenthal, Howard G., ed. (1998). *Favorite counseling and therapy techniques,* Accelerated Development (Philadelphia).

Rowan, Tim and O'Hanlon, Bill (1999). *Solution-oriented therapy for chronic and severe mental illness,* John Wiley and Sons (New York).

Schultheis, Gary M. (1998). *Brief therapy homework planner,* John Wiley and Sons (New York).

Selekman, Matthew D. (1997). *Solution focused therapy with children,* Guilford Press (New York).

Shapiro, Jerrold Lee, Peltz, Lawrence S., and Bernadett-Shapiro, Susan (1998). *Brief group treatment,* Brooks/Cole Publishing (Pacific Grove, CA).

Talmon, Moshe (1990). *Single session therapy,* Jossey-Bass Publishers (San Francisco).

Temple, Scott (1997). *Brief therapy for adolescent depression,* Professional Resource Press (Sarasota, FL).

Tucker, Jalie A., Donovan, Dennis M., and Marlatt, G. Alan, eds. (1999). *Changing addictive behavior,* Guilford Press (New York).

Valenstein, Elliot S. (1998). *Blaming the brain,* The Free Press (New York).

Walter, John L. and Peller, Jane E. (2000). *Recreating brief therapy,* W. W. Norton and Co. (New York).

Watters, Ethan and Ofshe, Richard (1999). *Therapy's delusions,* The Free Press (New York).

Weikel, William (1998). The telephone technique. In Howard G. Rosenthal (ed.), *Favorite counseling and therapy techniques* (pp. 189-190). Accelerated Development (Philadelphia).

White, Michael and Epston, David (1990). *Narrative means to therapeutic ends,* W. W. Norton (New York).

Index